The Classical Piano
Sheet Music Series

INTERMEDIATE
MOZART
FAVORITES

ISBN 978-1-70515-241-6

HAL•LEONARD®

Visit Hal Leonard Online at
www.halleonard.com

World headquarters, contact:
Hal Leonard
7777 West Bluemound Road
Milwaukee, WI 53213
Email: info@halleonard.com

In Europe, contact:
Hal Leonard Europe Limited
42 Wigmore Street
Marylebone, London, W1U 2RY
Email: info@halleonardeurope.com

In Australia, contact:
Hal Leonard Australia Pty. Ltd.
4 Lentara Court
Cheltenham, Victoria, 3192 Australia
Email: info@halleonard.com.au

Contents

Air in A-flat Major

K. Anh. 109b, Nr. 8 (15ff)

Wolfgang Amadeus Mozart
(1756–1791)

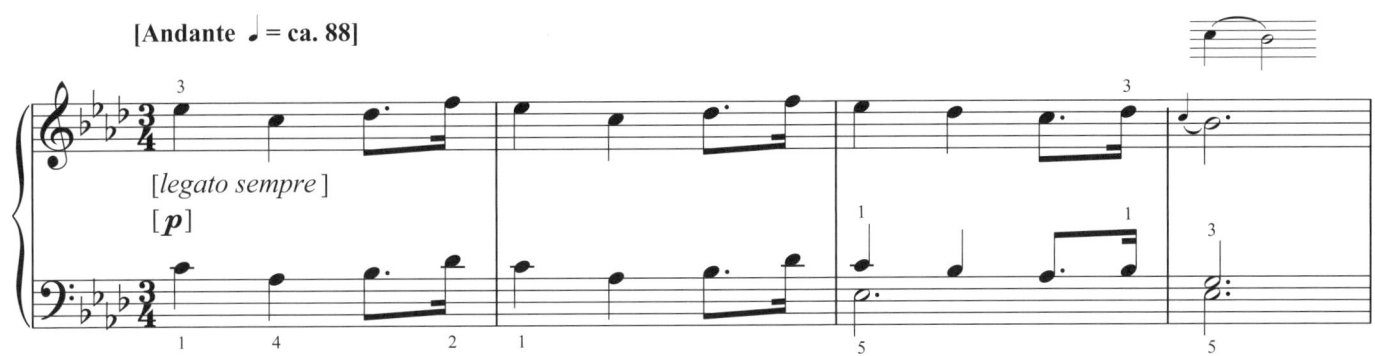

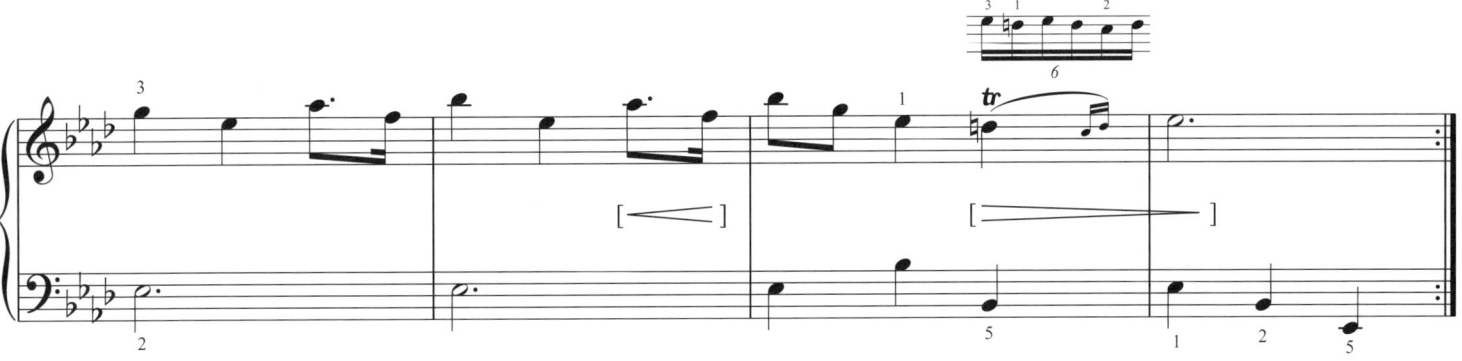

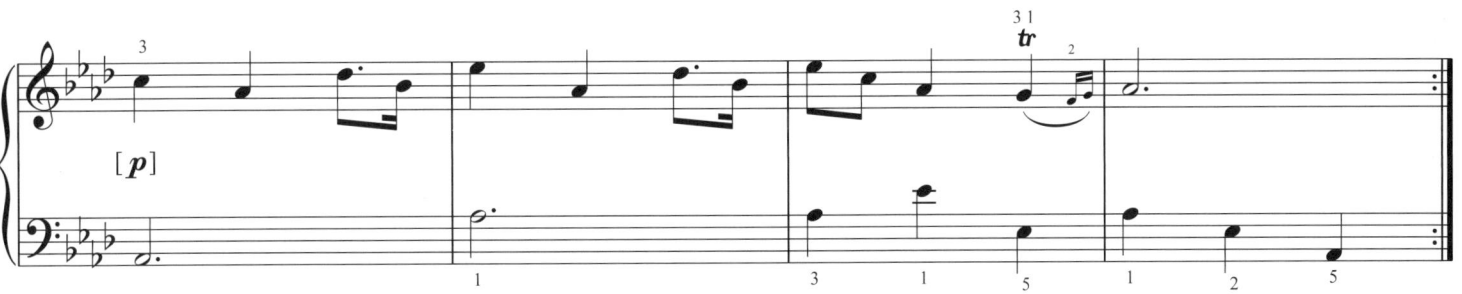

Adagio in C Major for Glass Harmonica
K. 356 (617a)

Wolfgang Amadeus Mozart
(1756–1791)

Allegro in B-flat Major
K. 3

Wolfgang Amadeus Mozart
(1756–1791)

Allegro [♩ = ca. 120–126]

Allegro in F Major
K. 1c

Wolfgang Amadeus Mozart
(1756–1781)

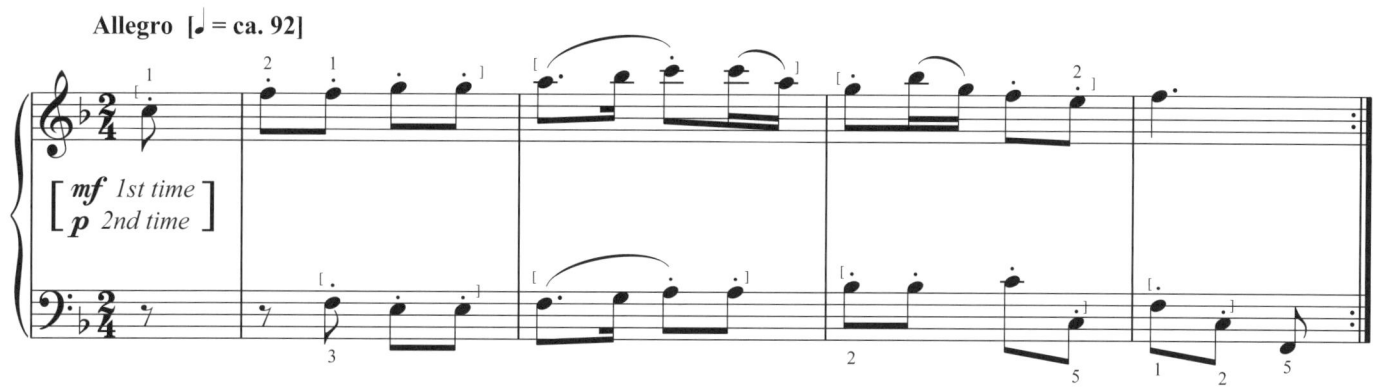

Allegro in F Major

K. Anh. 109b, No. 1 (15a)

Wolfgang Amadeus Mozart
(1756–1781)

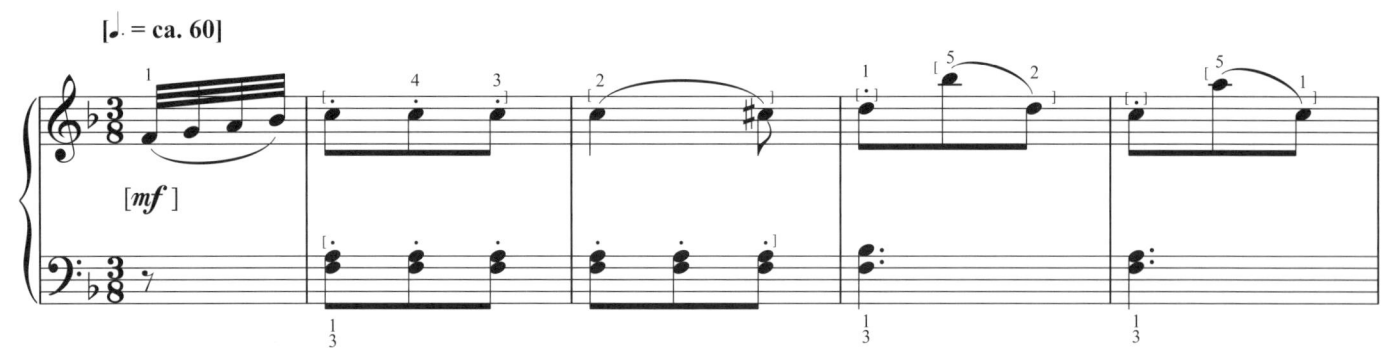

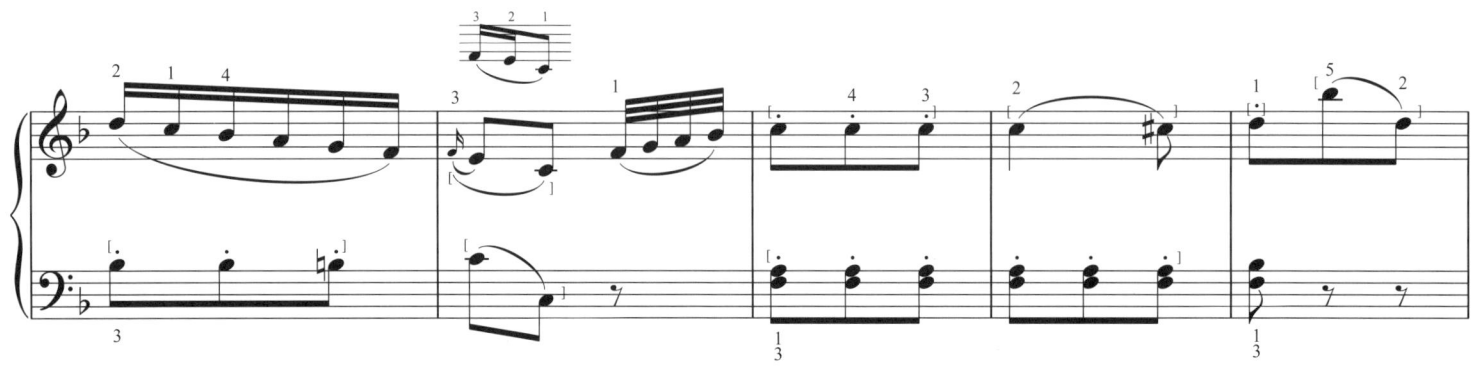

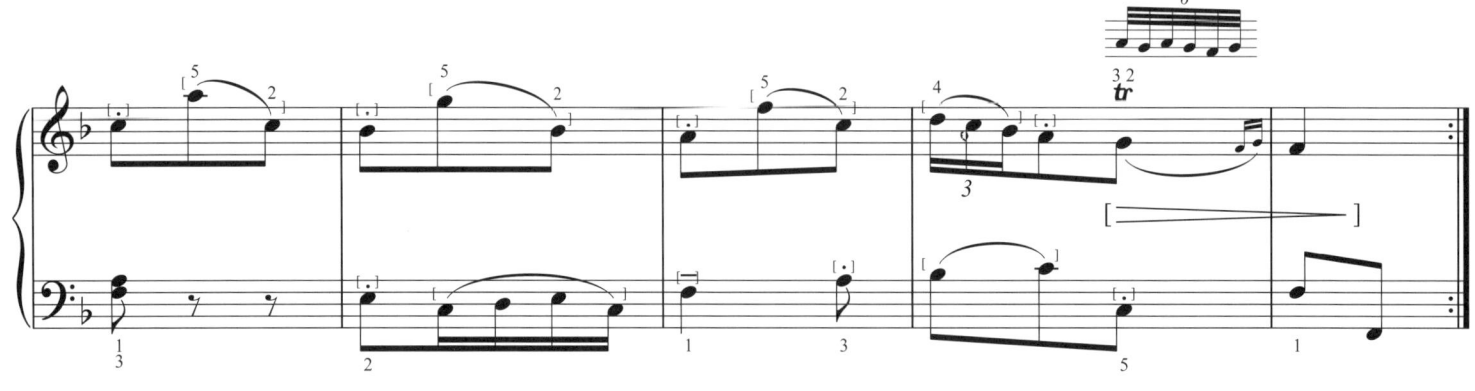

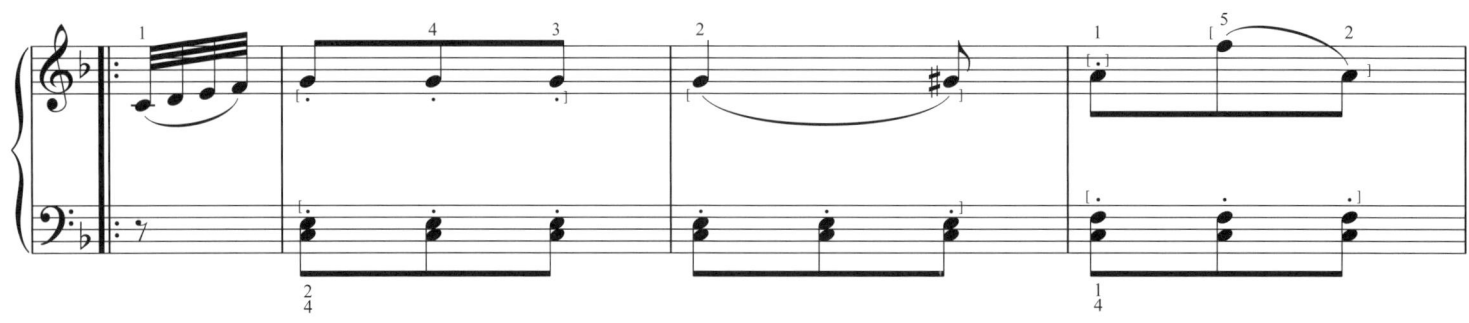

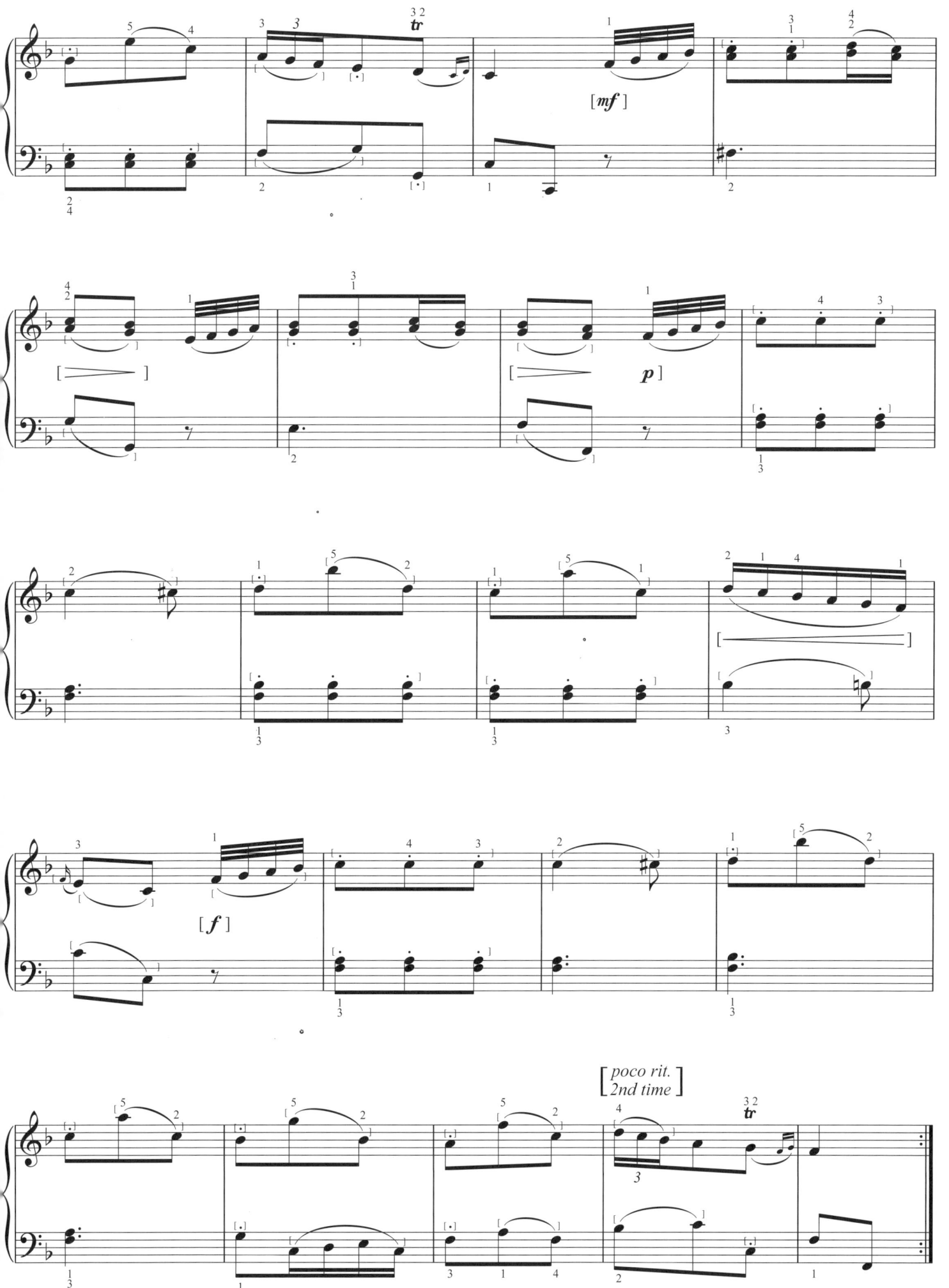

Andante in C Major
K. 1a

Wolfgang Amadeus Mozart
(1756–1791)

Andante [♩ = ca. 56]

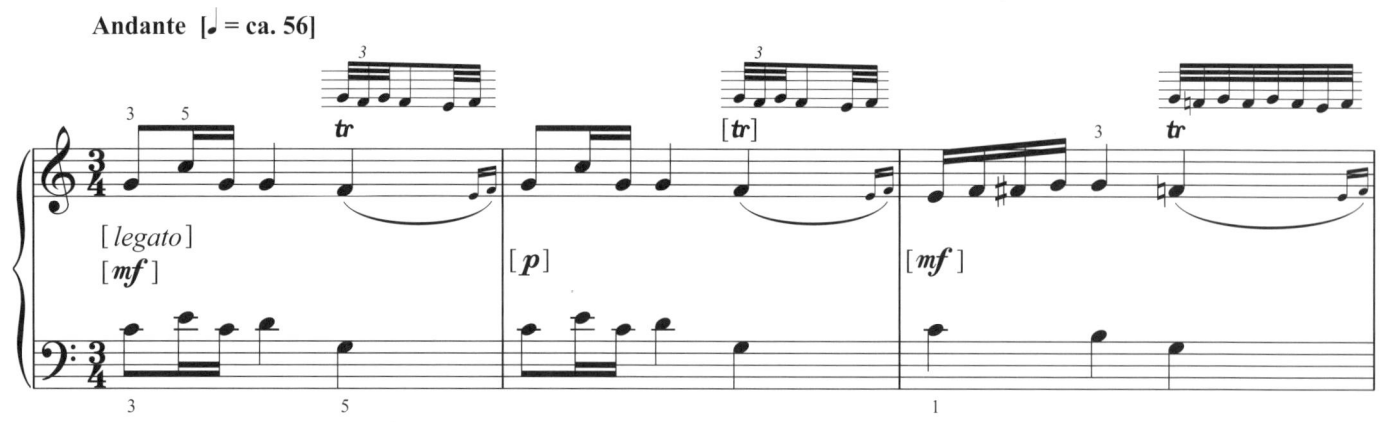

Andante in E-flat Major
K. 15mm

Wolfgang Amadeus Mozart
(1756–1791)

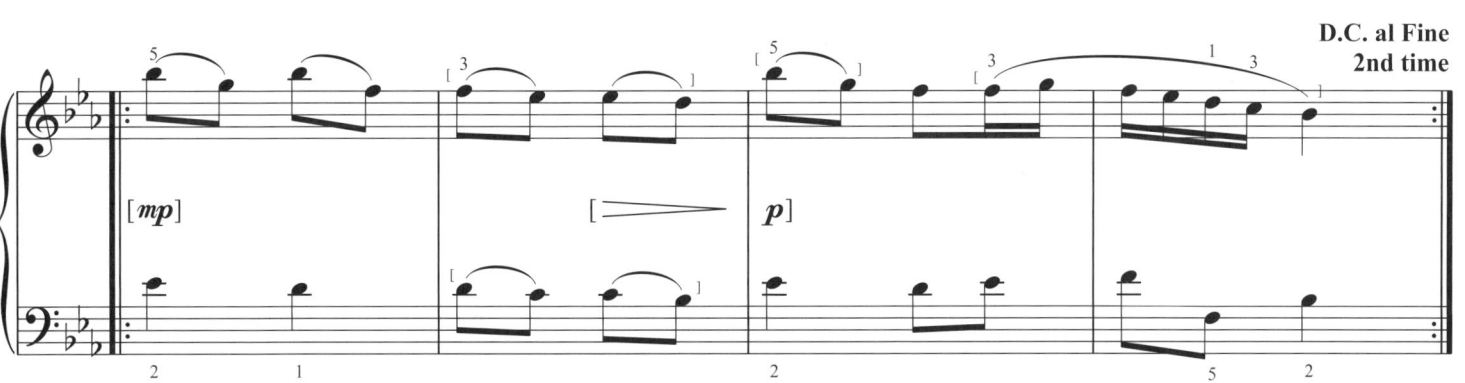

Andantino* in E-flat Major
K. 236 (588b)

Wolfgang Amadeus Mozart
(1756–1791)

* "Non vi turbate" from Christoph Willibald Gluck's *Alceste.*

Contradance in G Major
K. 15e

Wolfgang Amadeus Mozart
(1756–1791)

[Allegro ♩ = ca. 108]

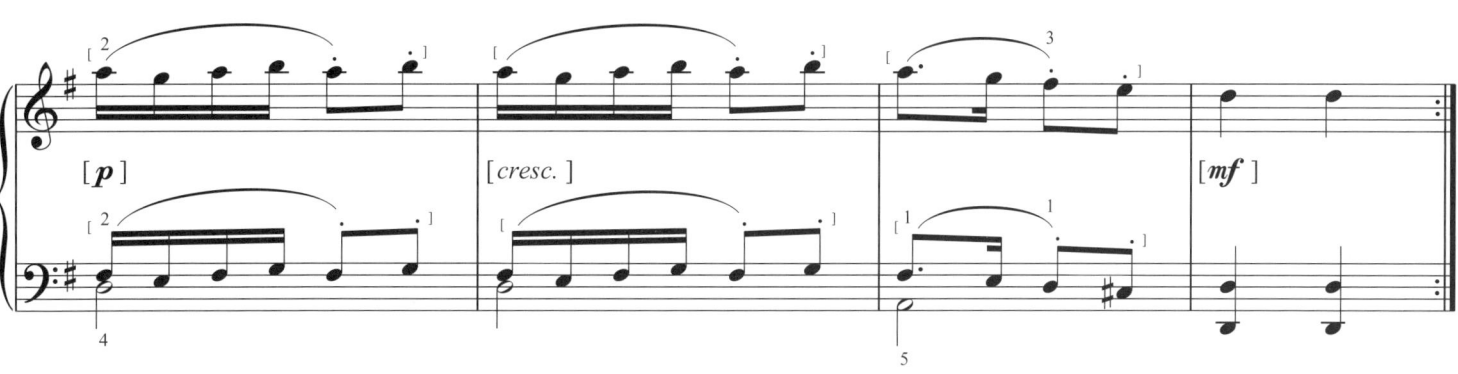

Contradance in D Major
"The Thunderstorm"
K. 534

Wolfgang Amadeus Mozart
(1756–1791)

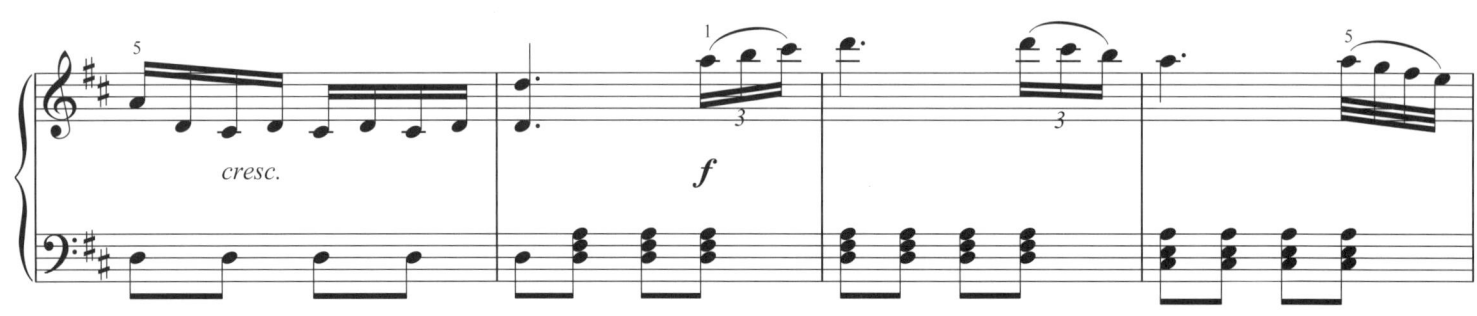

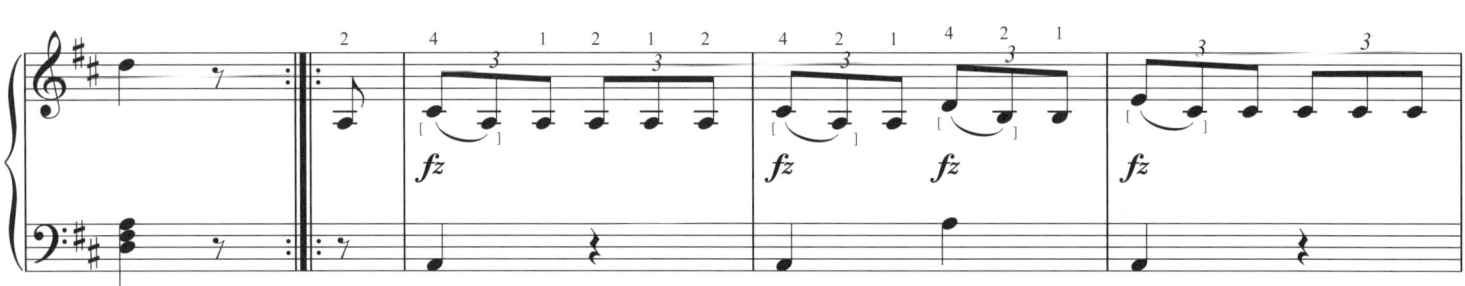

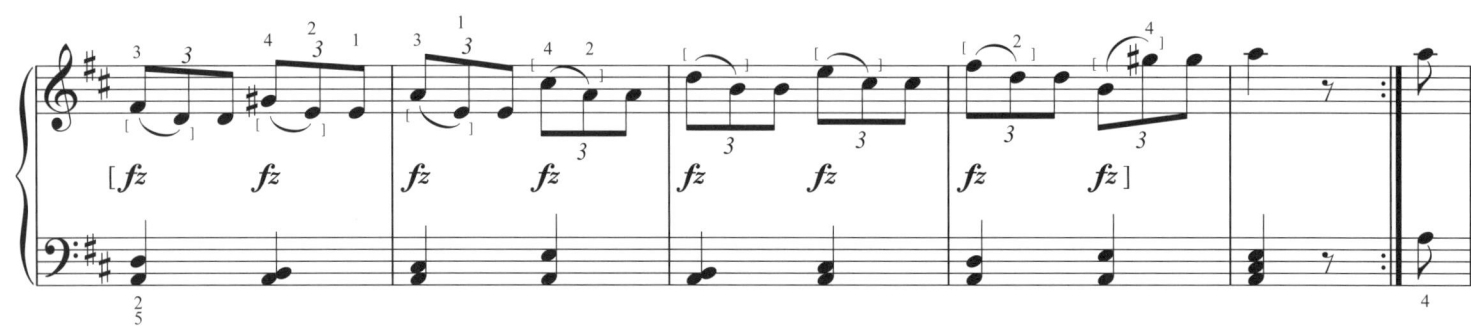

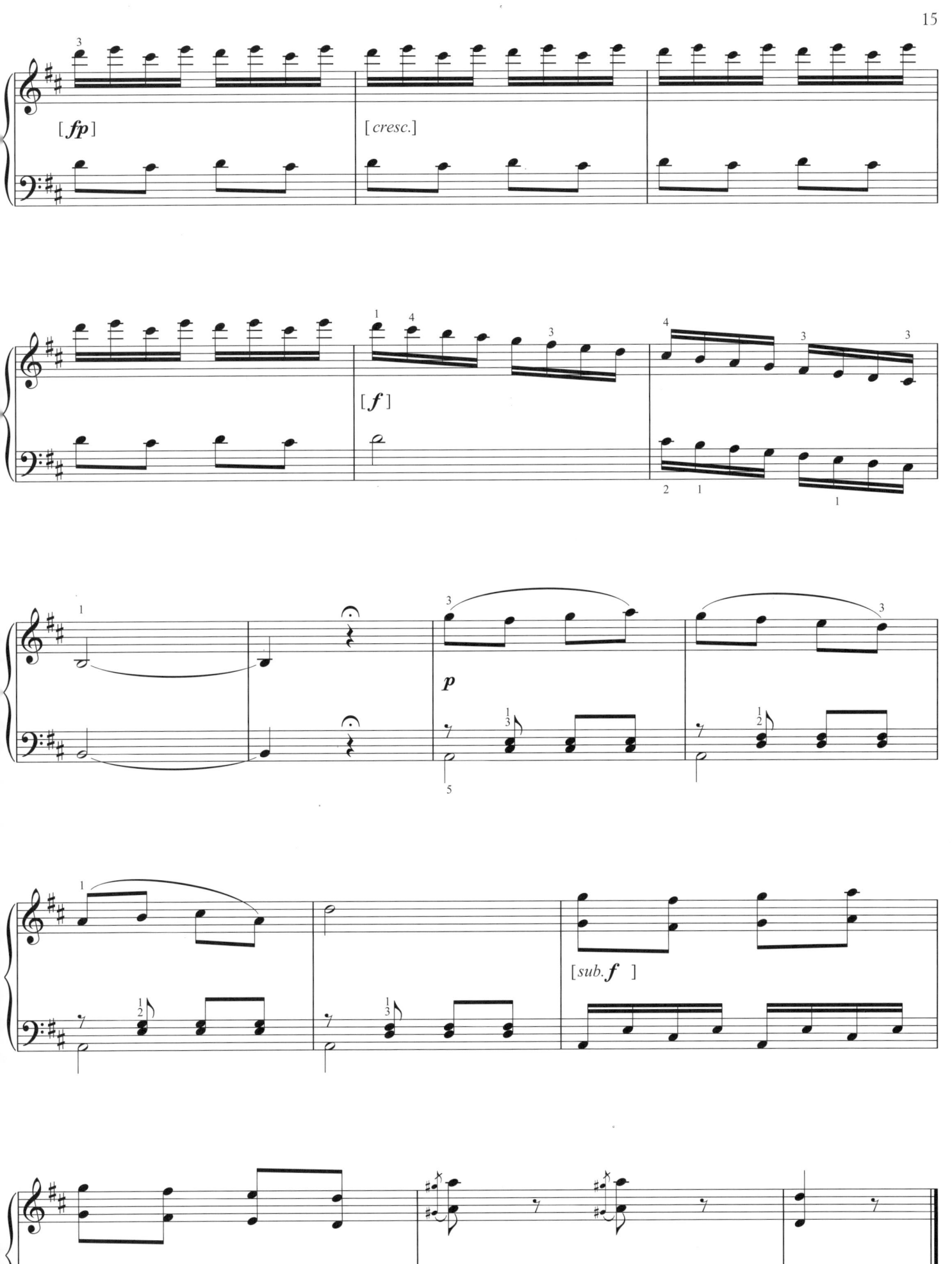

for Johann Rudolf Graf Czernin

Contradance in G Major
K. 269b

Wolfgang Amadeus Mozart
(1756–1791)

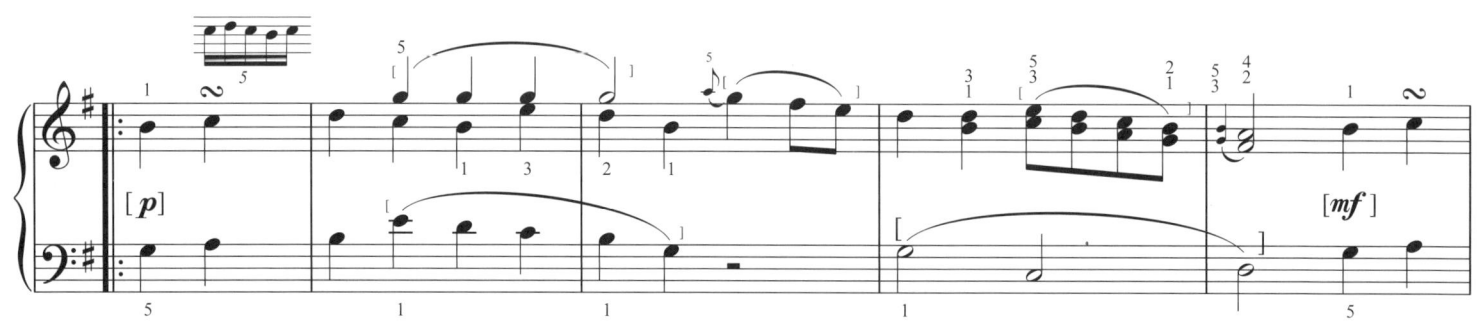

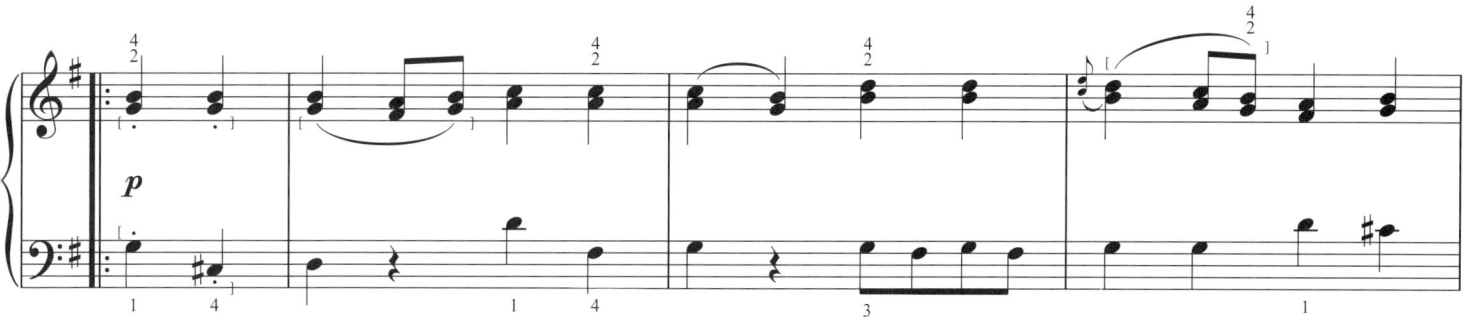

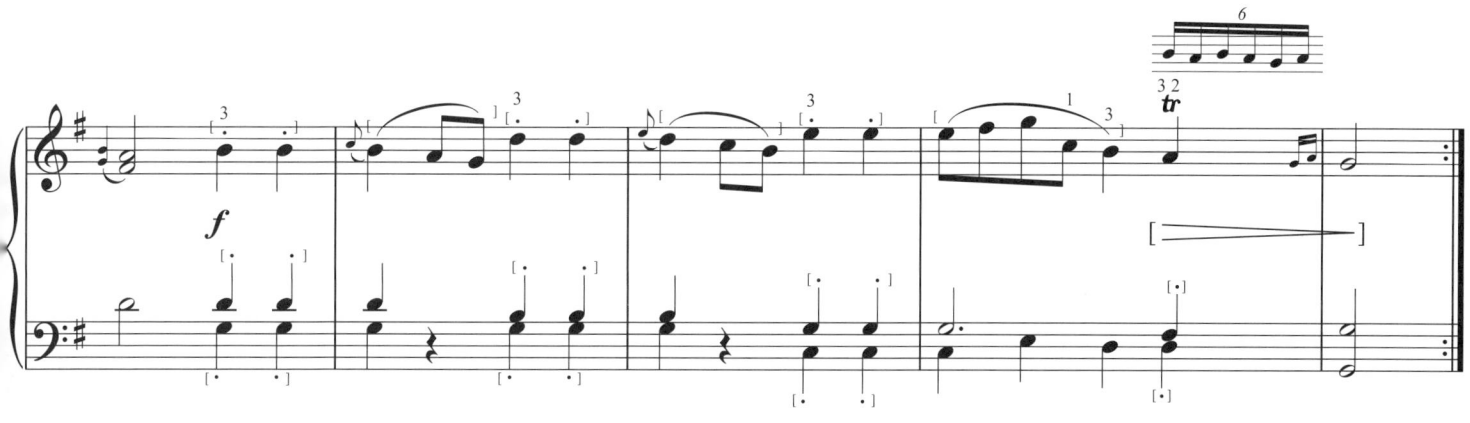

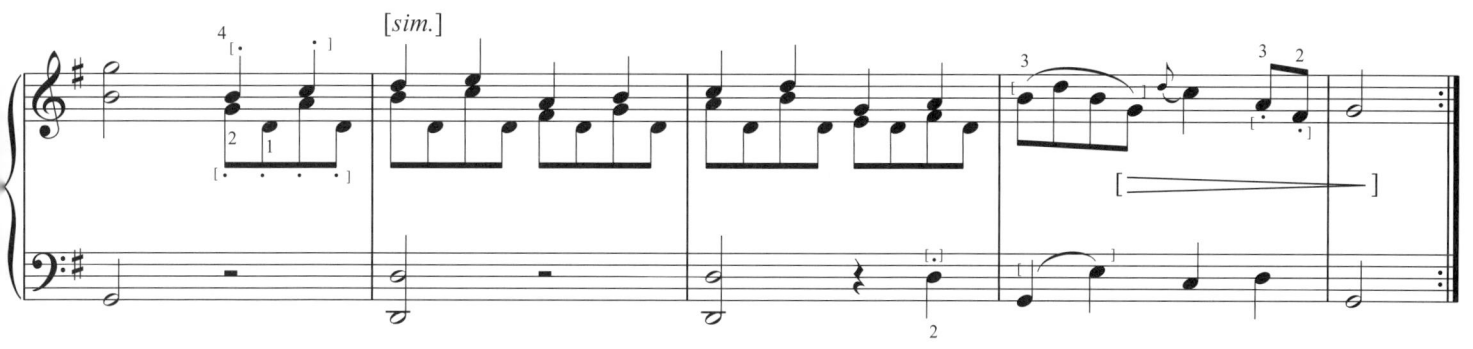

Funeral March for
Signor Maestro Contrapunto

K. 453a

Wolfgang Amadeus Mozart
(1756–1791)

Eight Variations
on a March from *Les mariages samnites*
K. 352

Wolfgang Amadeus Mozart
(1756–1791)

THEMA
[Maestoso]

VAR. III

VAR. IV

VAR. VII
Adagio

VAR. VIII

Allegro

Gavotte in F Major

from *Les petits riens*
K. Anh. 10 (299b)

Wolfgang Amadeus Mozart
(1756–1791)

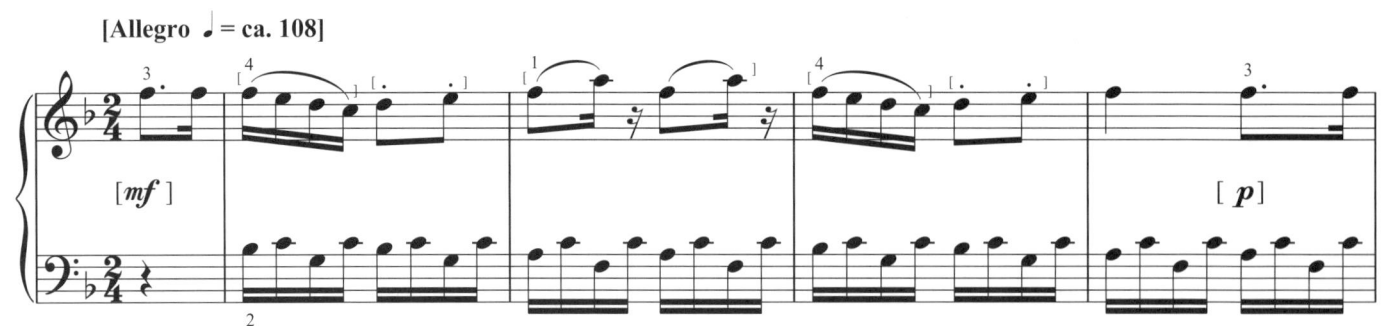

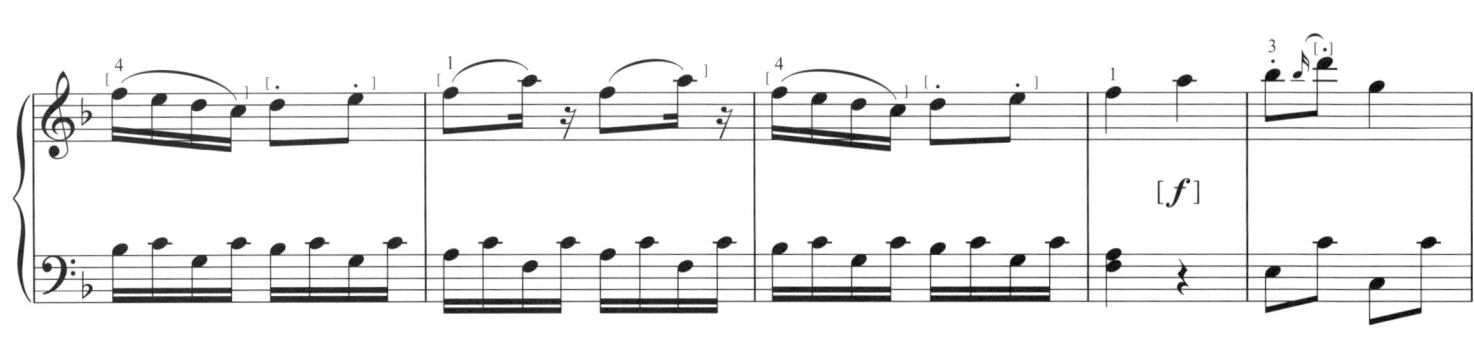

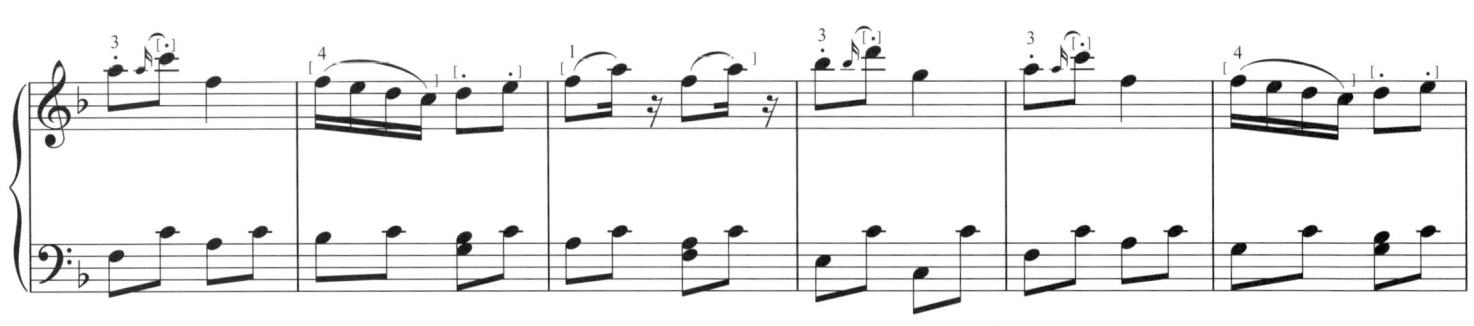

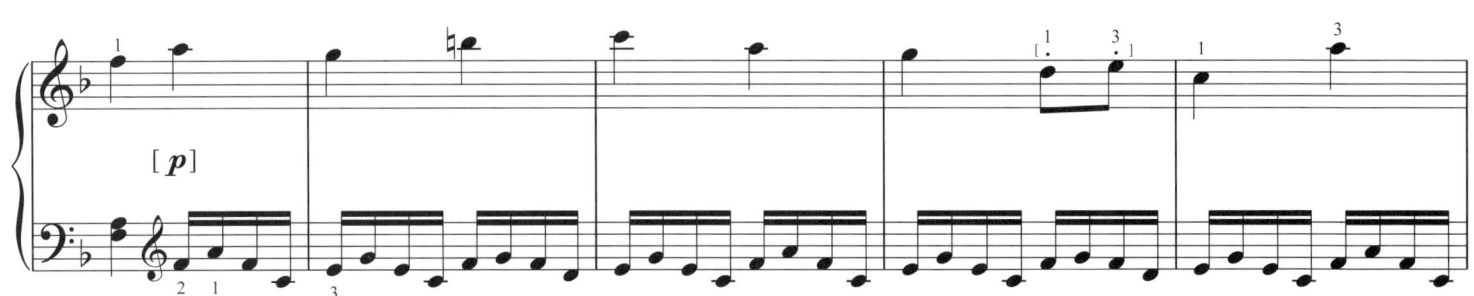

Larghetto in F Major
K. deest

Wolfgang Amadeus Mozart
(1756–1791)

German Dance in C Major
K. 605, No. 3

Wolfgang Amadeus Mozart
(1756–1791)

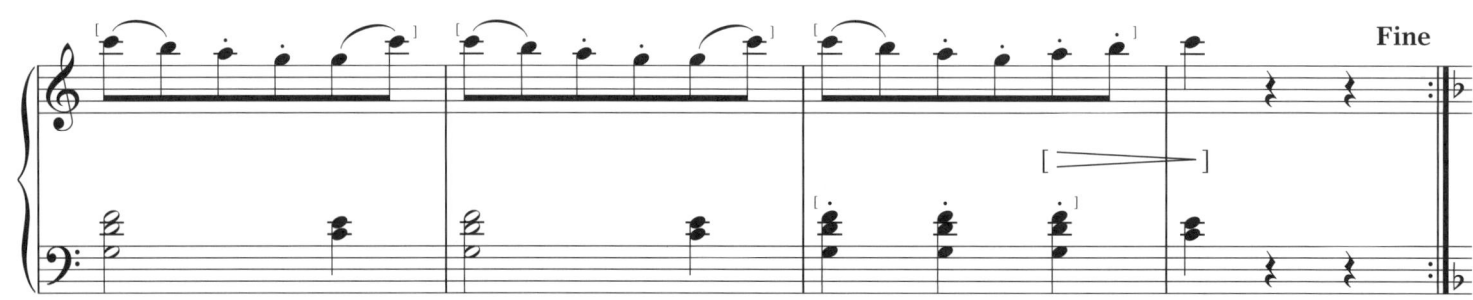

Trio (The Sleighride)

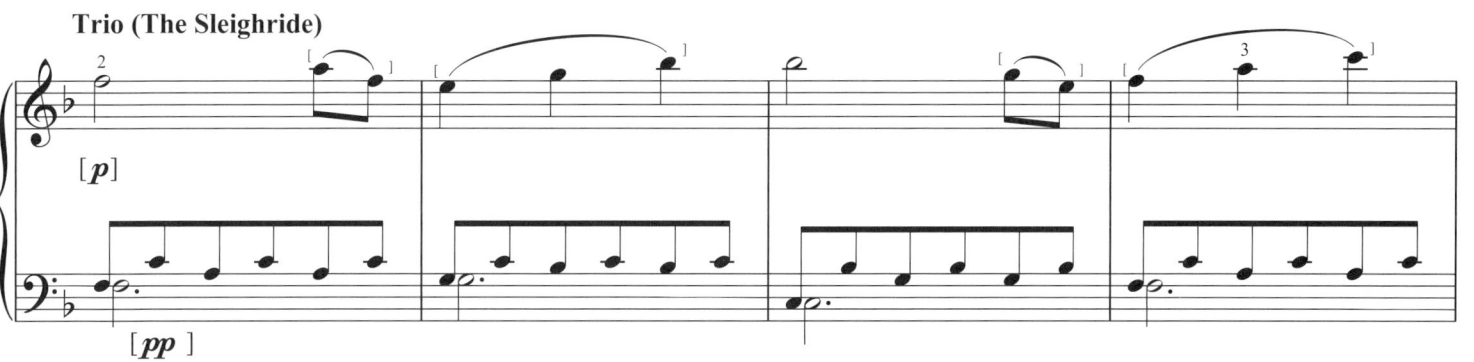

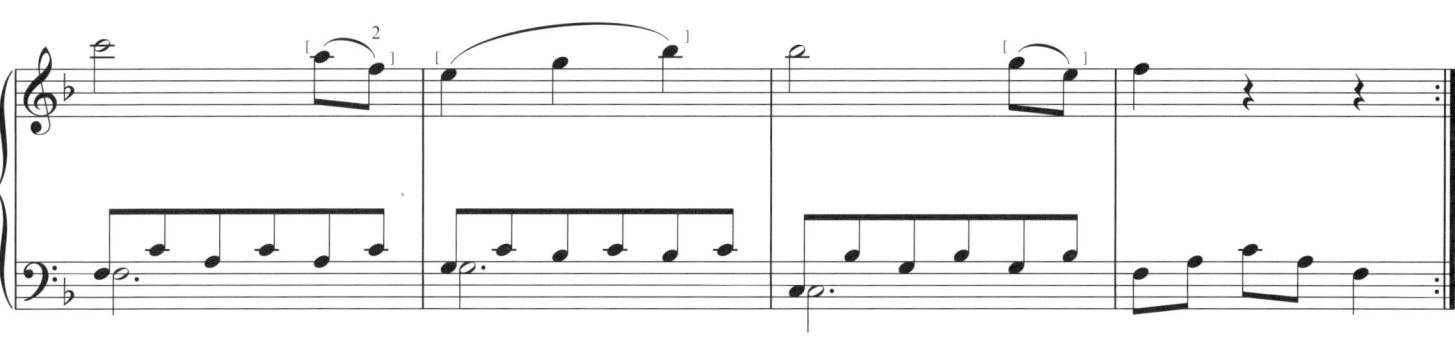

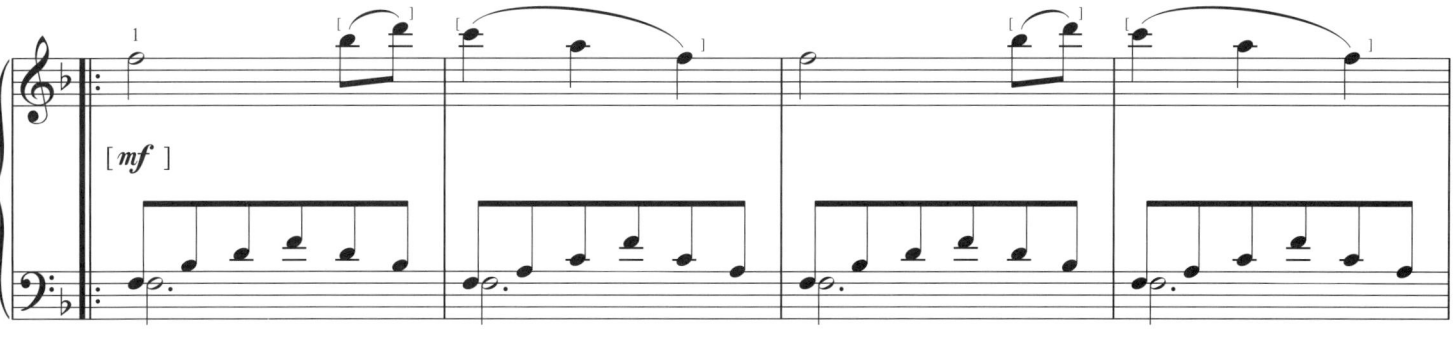

D.C. al Fine
second time

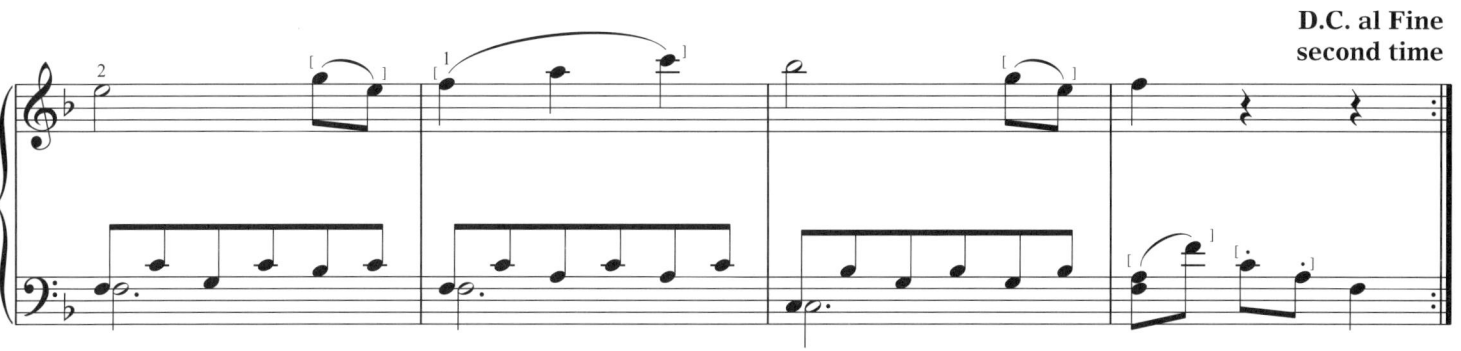

Minuet in B-flat Major
K. 15pp

Wolfgang Amadeus Mozart
(1756–1791)

[Andantino ♩ = ca. 112]

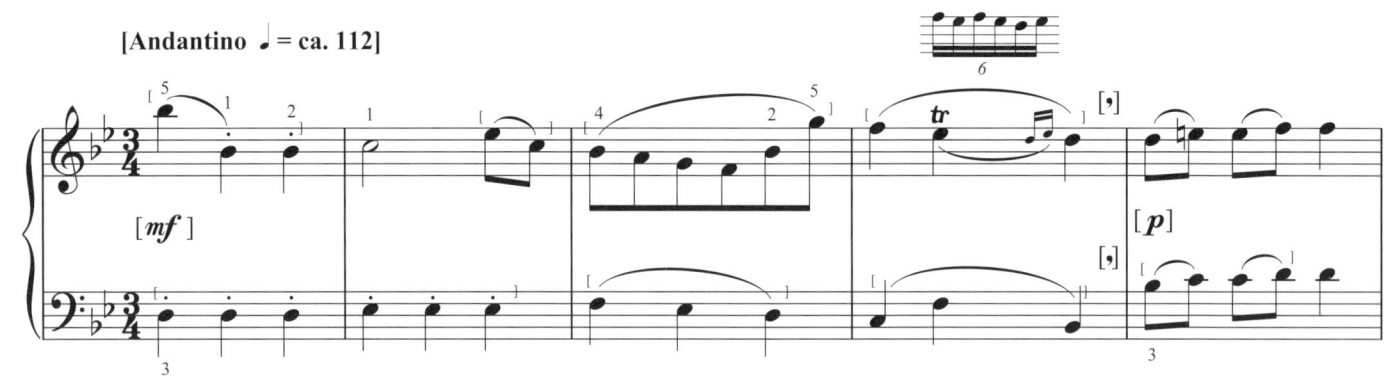

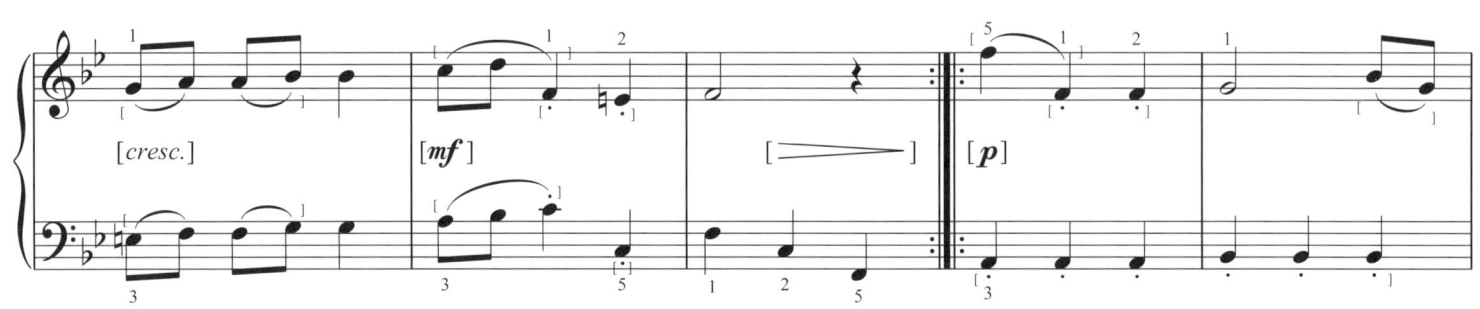

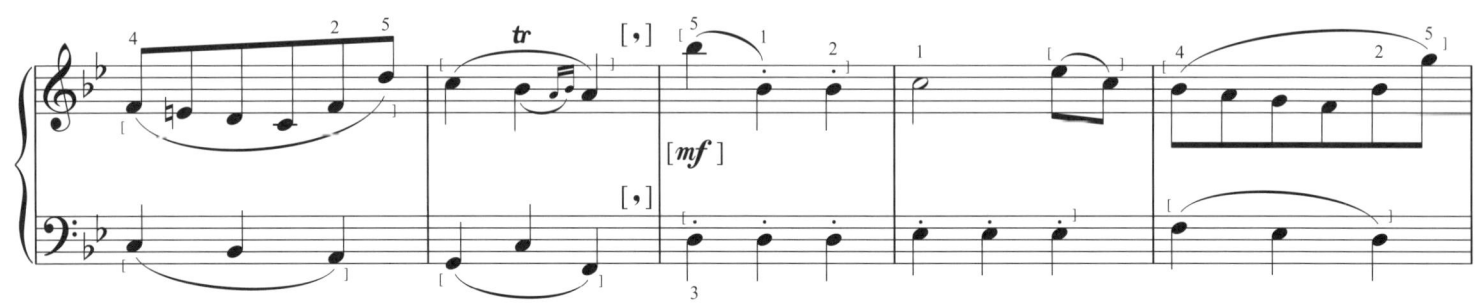

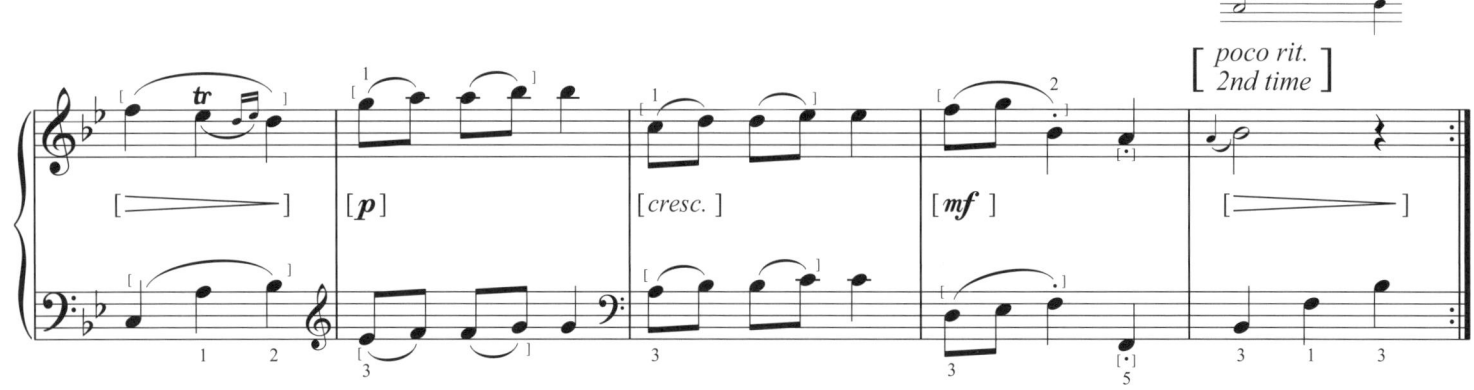

Minuet in C Major
K. 6 (I)

Wolfgang Amadeus Mozart
(1756–1791)

[Andante moderato ♩ = ca. 100]

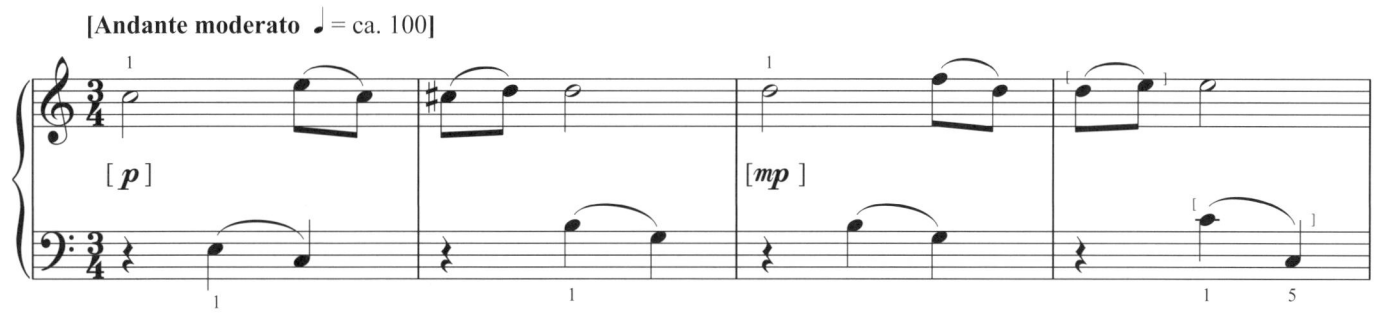

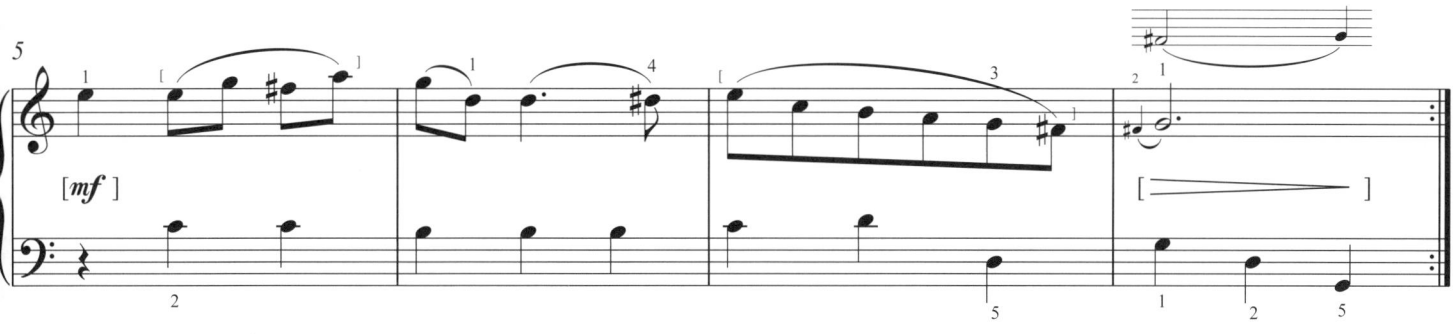

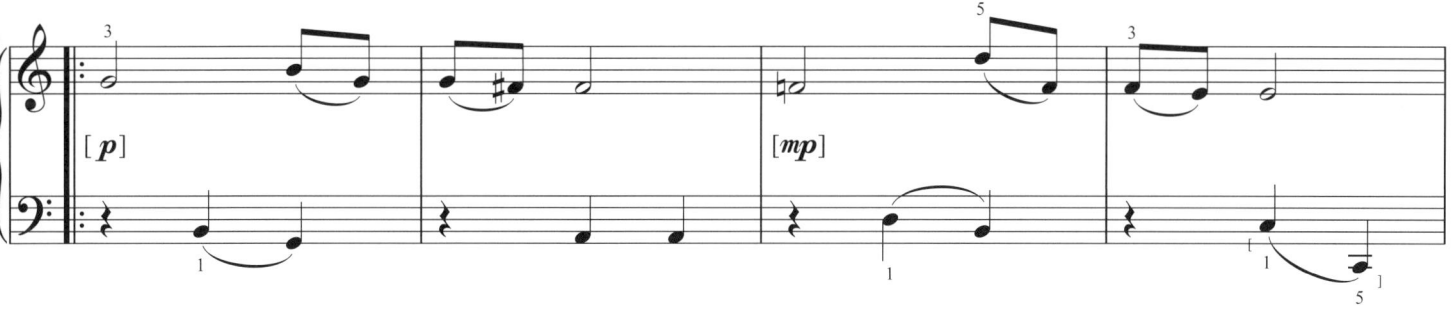

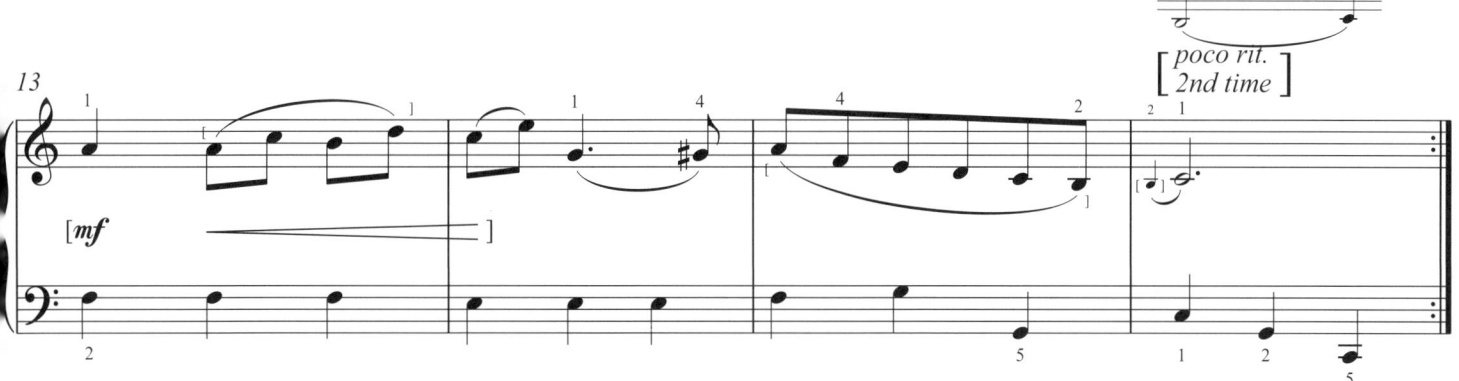

Minuet in D Major
K. 7

Wolfgang Amadeus Mozart
(1756–1791)

Minuet in D Major
K. 94 (73h)

Wolfgang Amadeus Mozart
(1756–1791)

In the manuscript. We have raised the lower voice one octave to facilitate this passage.

Minuet in E-flat Major
K. 15qq

Wolfgang Amadeus Mozart
(1756–1791)

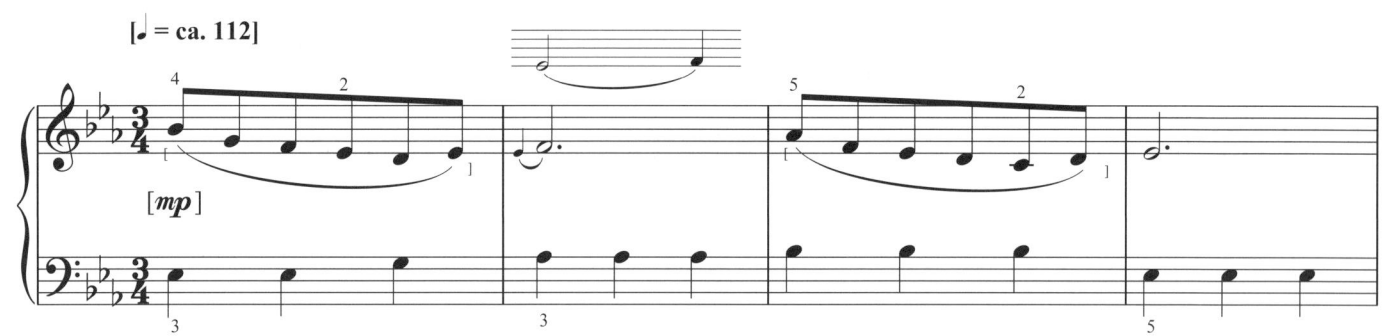

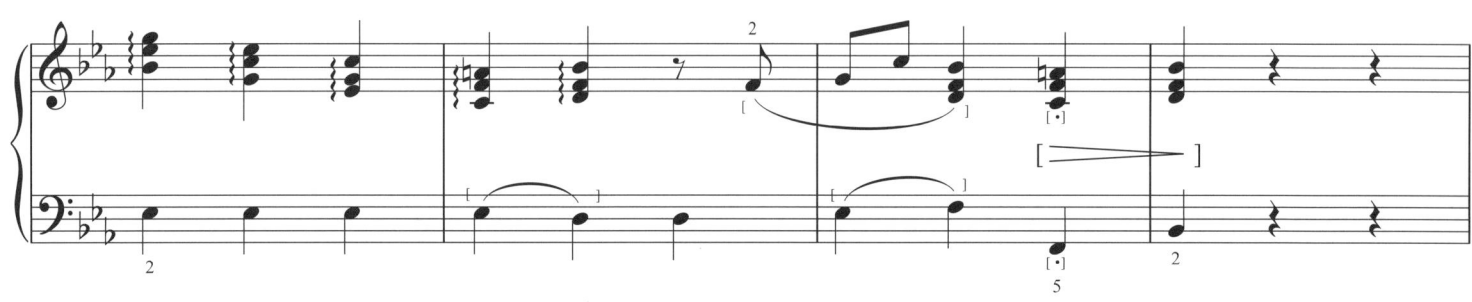

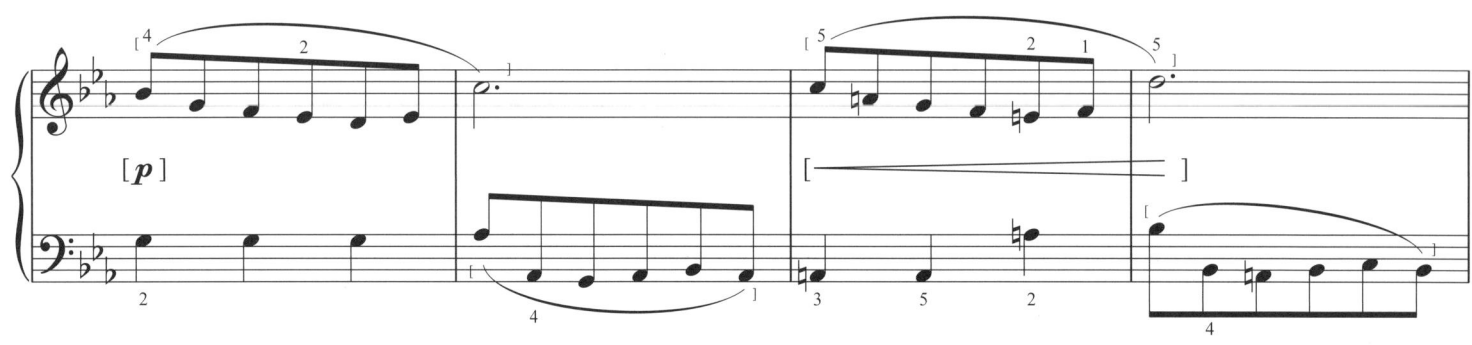

Minuet in F Major
K. 1d

Wolfgang Amadeus Mozart
(1756–1791)

Minuet in F Major
K. 2

Wolfgang Amadeus Mozart
(1756–1791)

[Allegretto ♩ = ca. 108]

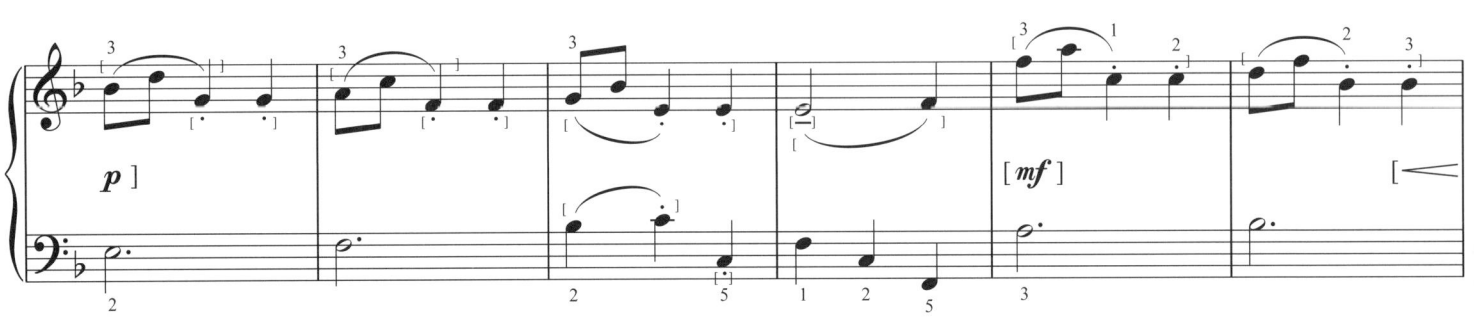

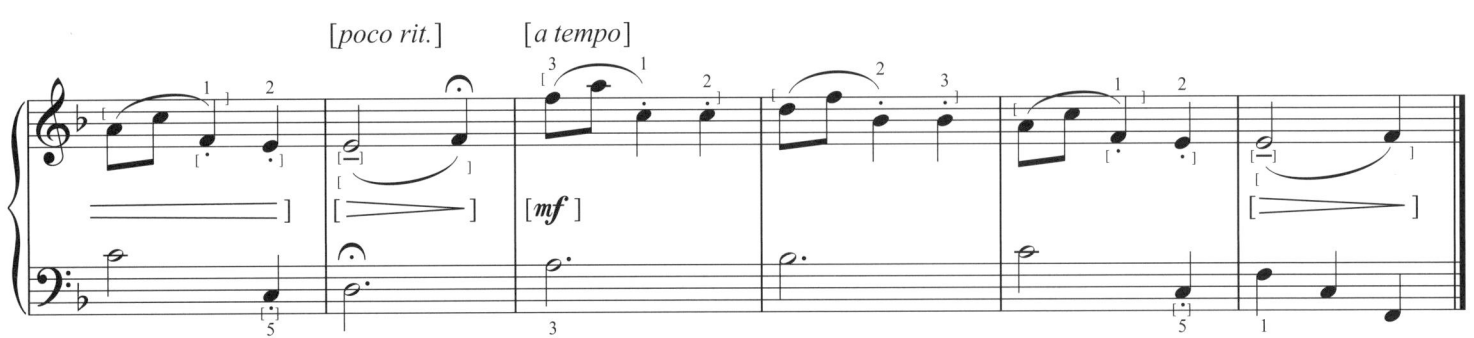

Minuet in F Major
K. 5

Wolfgang Amadeus Mozart
(1756–1791)

Minuet in F Major
K. 6 (II)

Wolfgang Amadeus Mozart
(1756–1791)

Minuet in G Major
K. 15c

Wolfgang Amadeus Mozart
(1756–1791)

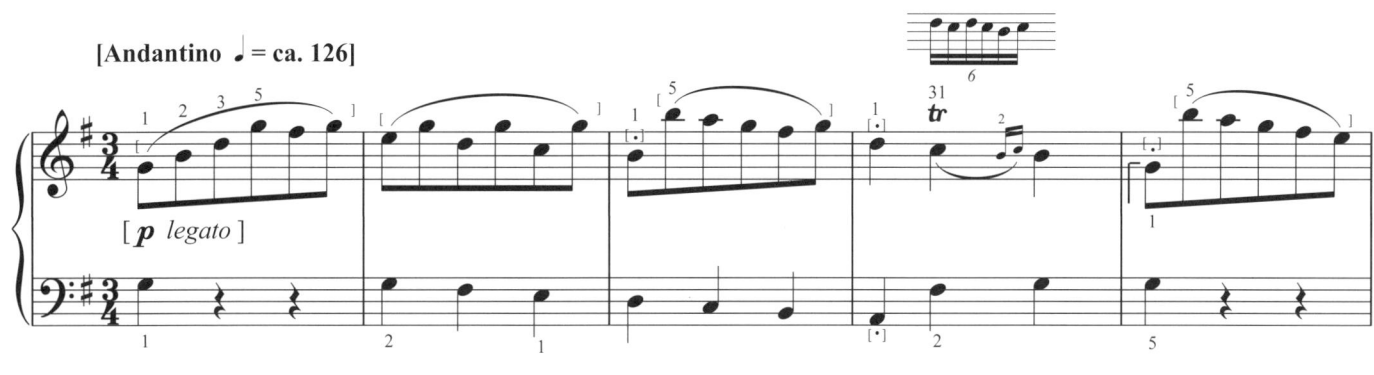

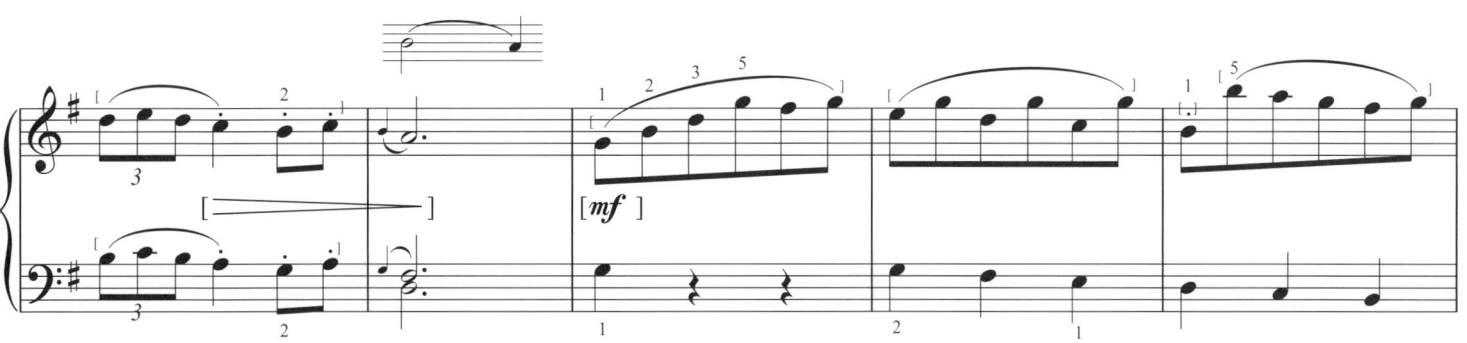

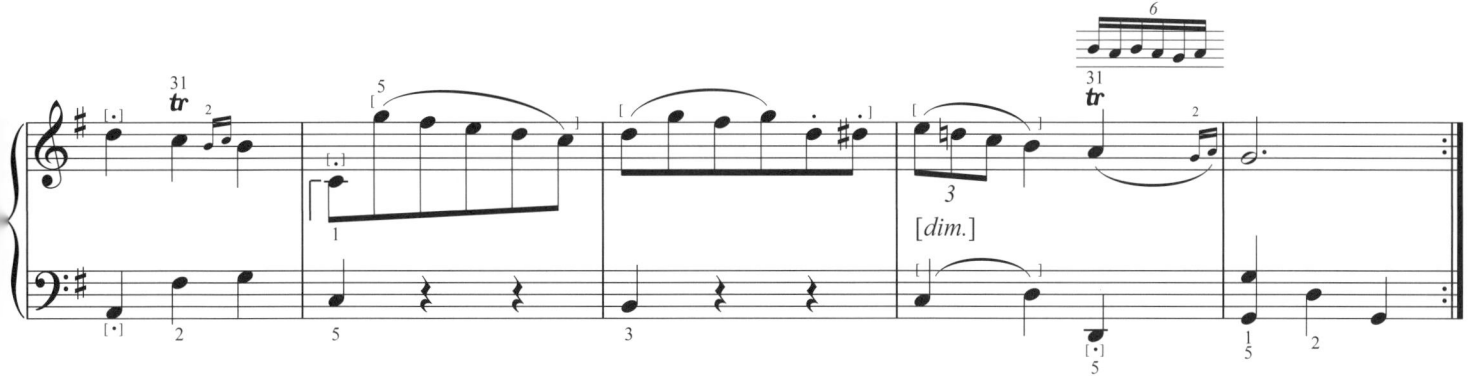

Minuet in G Major
K. 15y

Wolfgang Amadeus Mozart
(1756–1791)

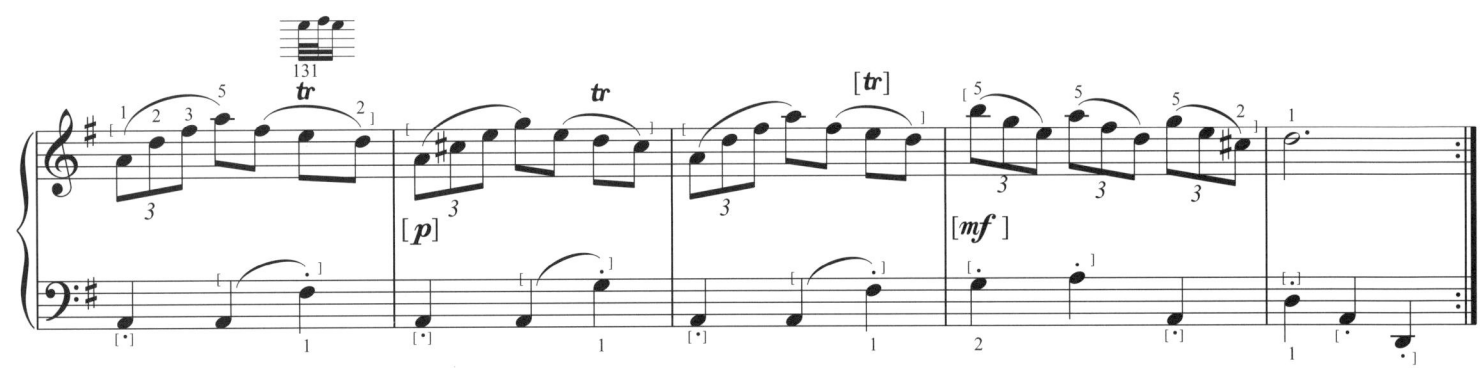

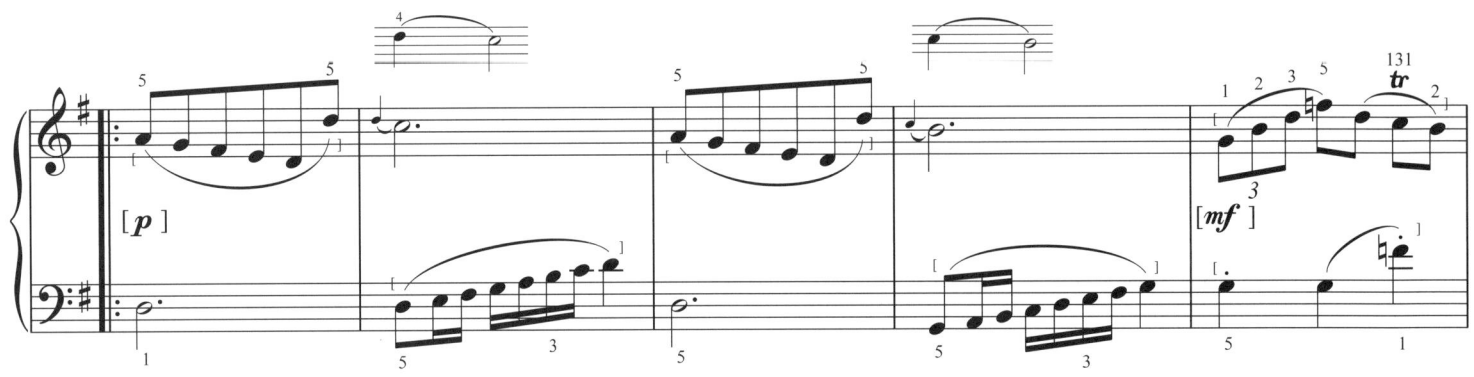

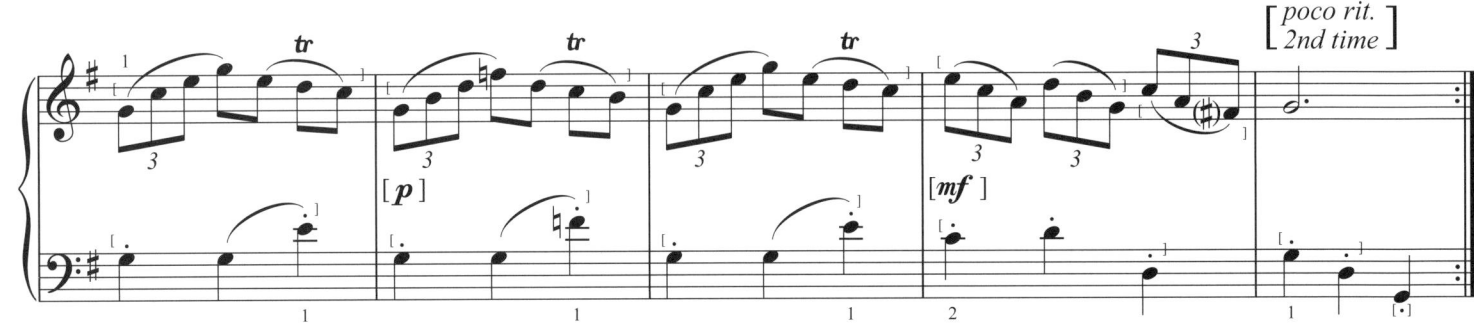

Rondo in F Major

K. 15hh

Wolfgang Amadeus Mozart
(1756–1791)

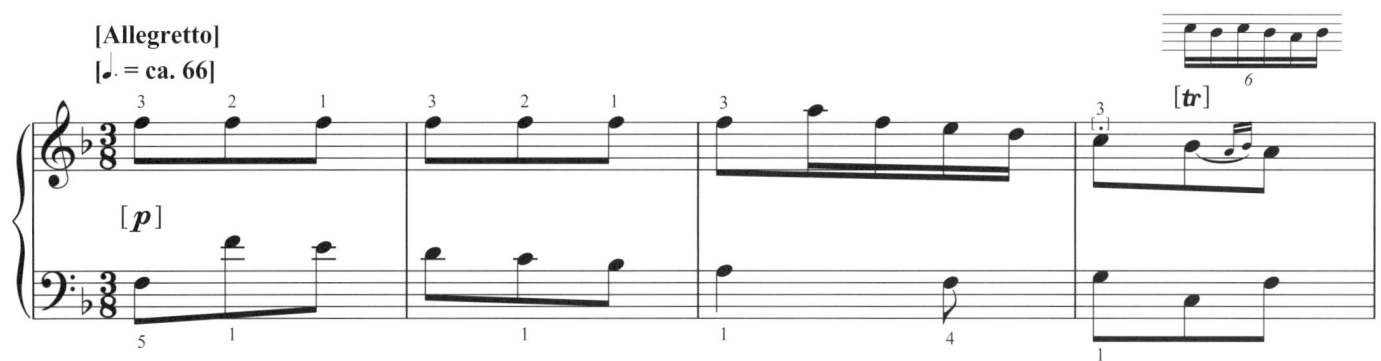

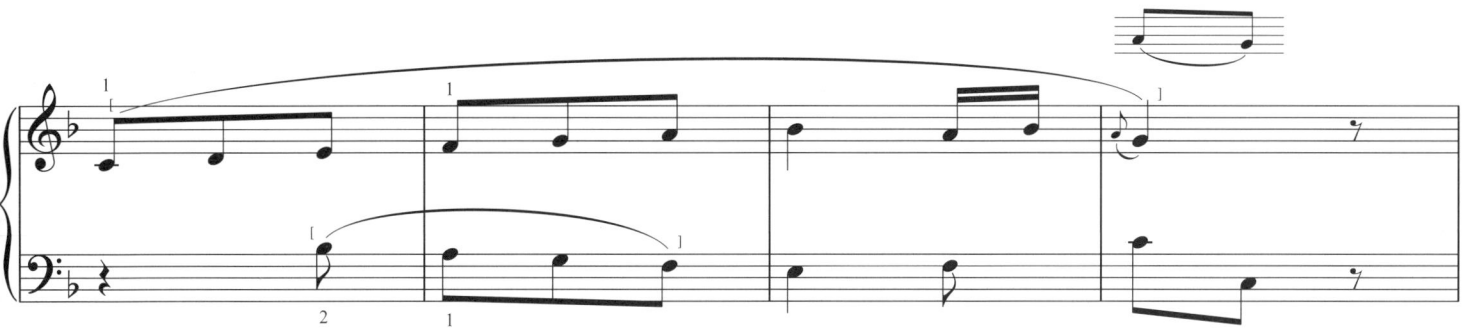

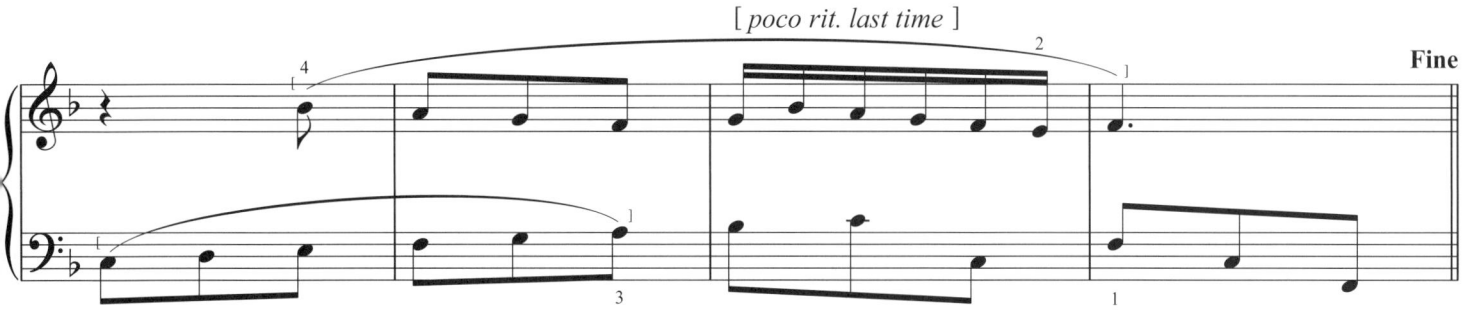

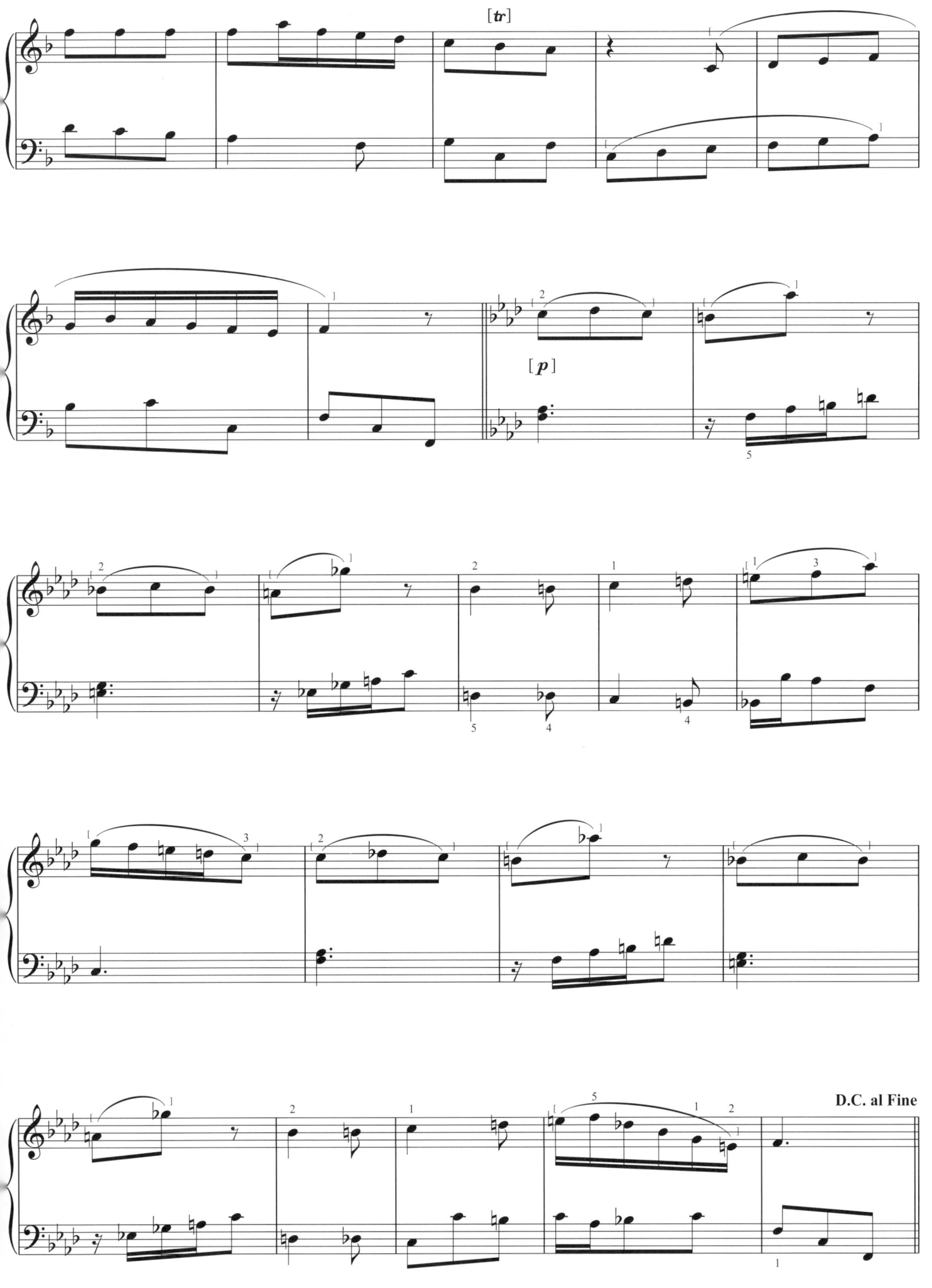

Minuet in G Major
K. 1e/f

Wolfgang Amadeus Mozart
(1756–1791)

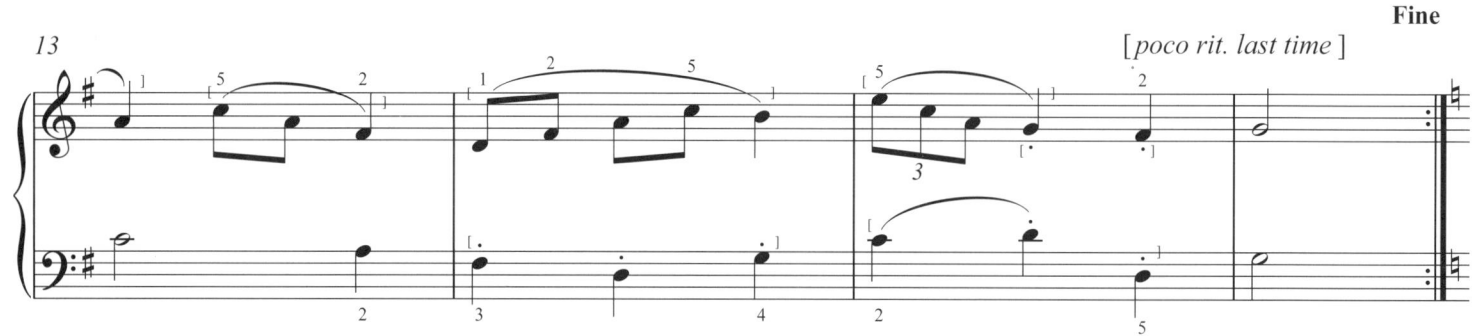

Trio

[*f* 1st time]
[*p* 2nd time]

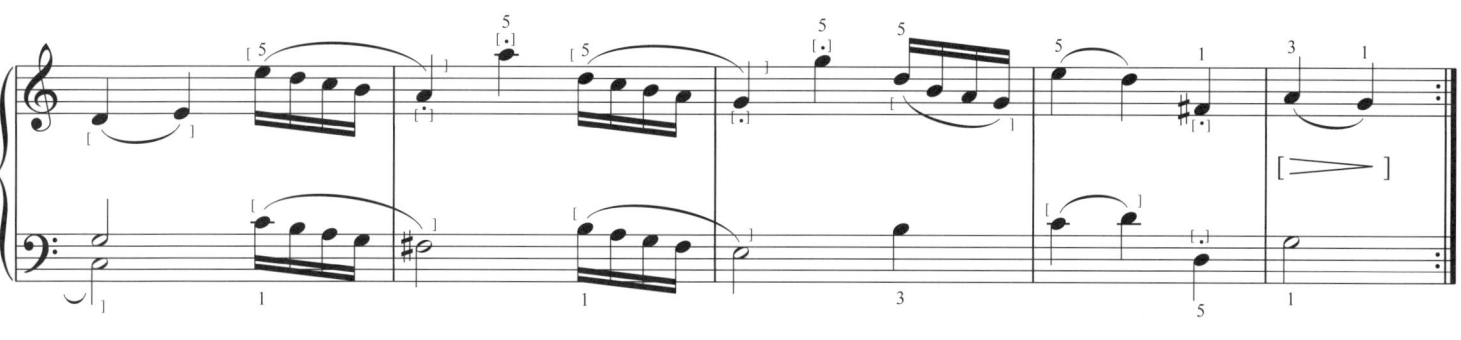

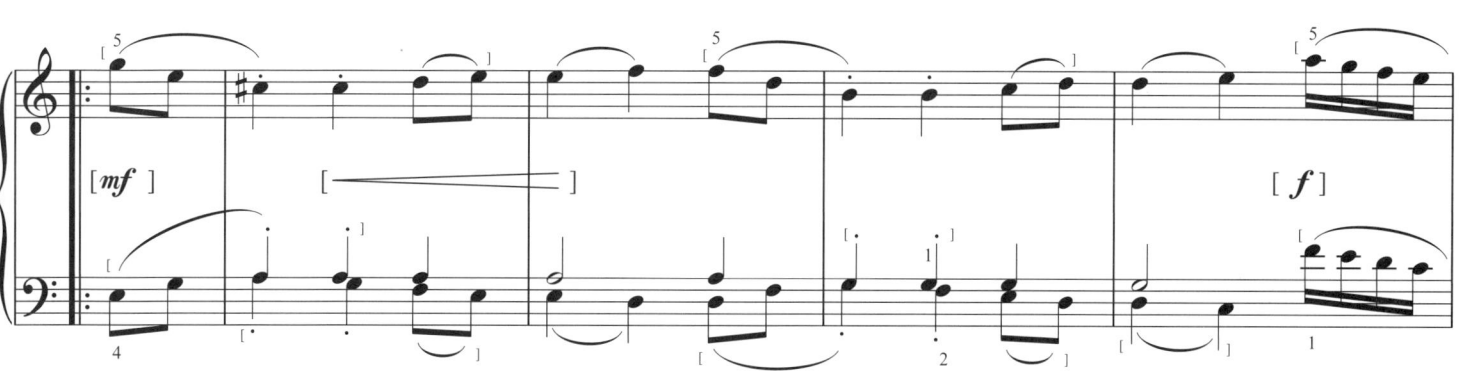

[*mf*]

[*f*]

D.C. al Fine
second time

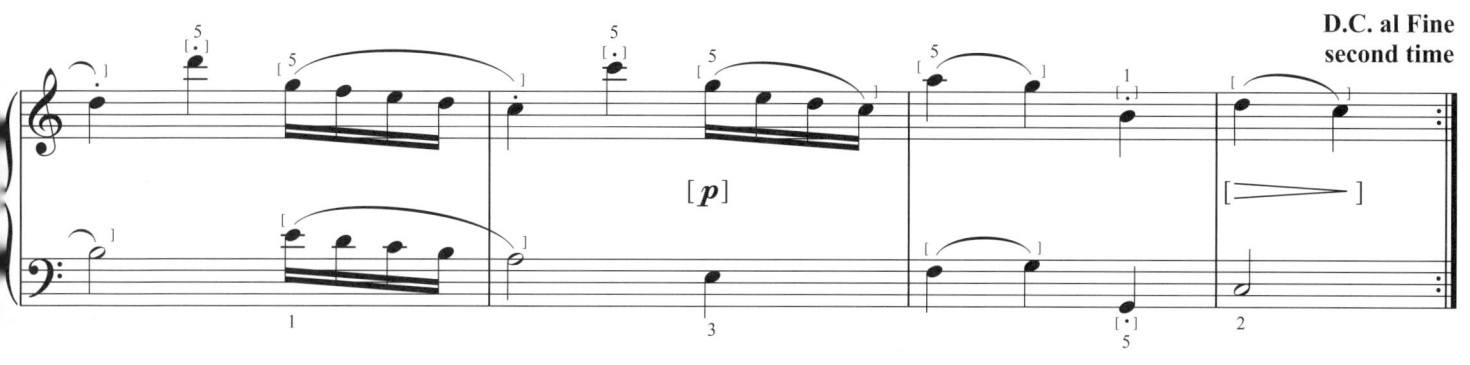

[*p*]

Piece for Clavier in F Major
K. 33B

Wolfgang Amadeus Mozart
(1756–1791)

[*poco rit. 2nd time*]

Rondo in C Major
K. 334 (320b)

Wolfgang Amadeus Mozart
(1756–1791)

[Allegro ♩. = 92]

Sonata in C Major
"Sonata facile"
K. 545

Wolfgang Amadeus Mozart
(1756–1791)

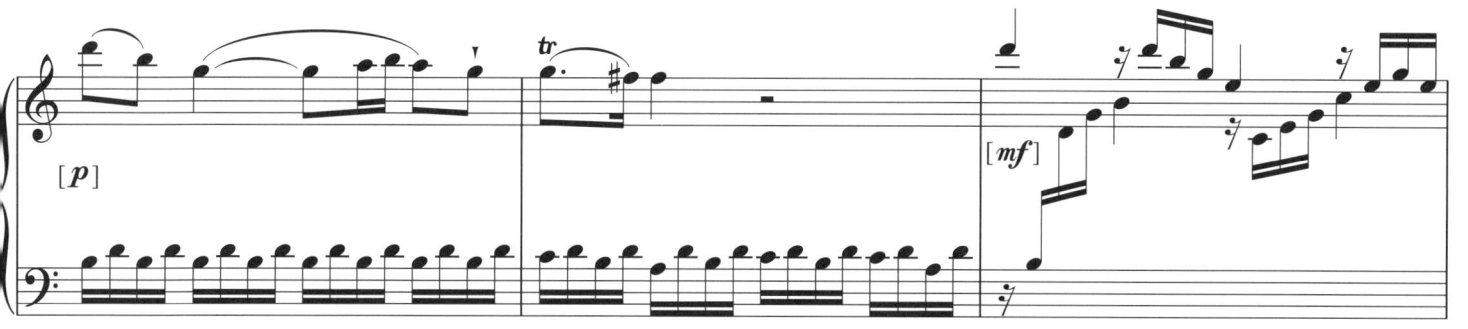

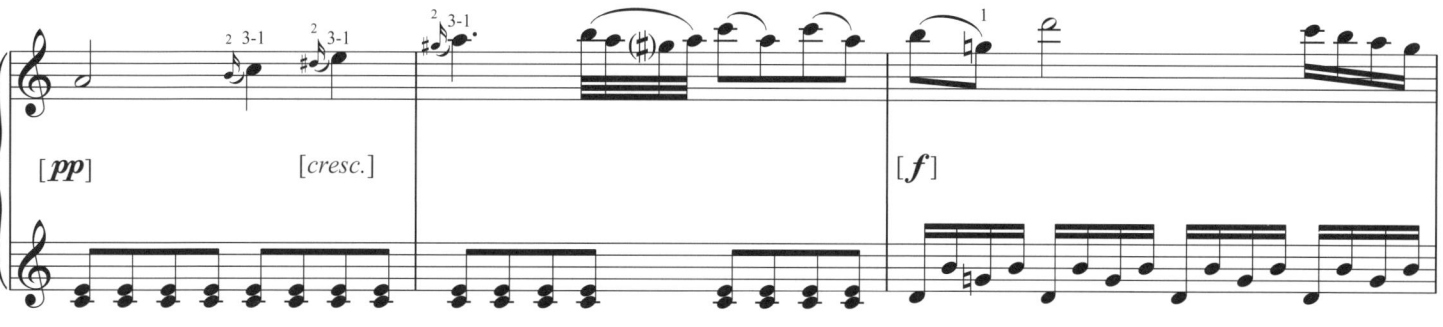

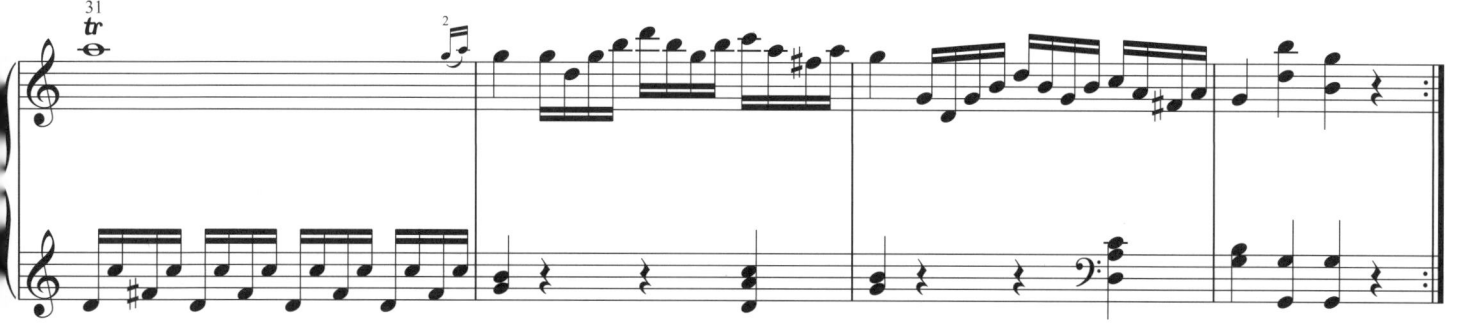

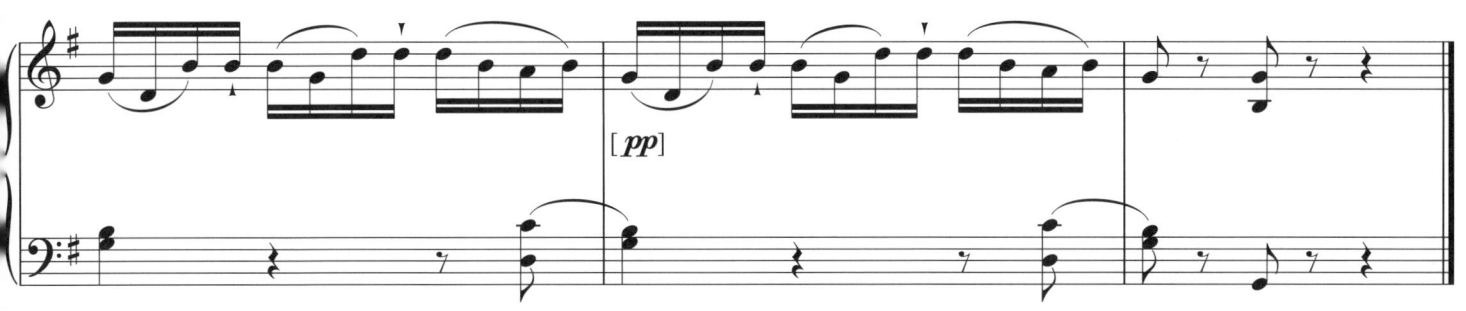

Rondo

Allegretto

Six Variations
on "Mio caro Adone"
K. 180

Wolfgang Amadeus Mozart
(1756–1791)

VAR. II

VAR. III

VAR. IV

VAR. V

Adagio

VAR. VI
Allegretto

Twelve Variations
on "Ah, vous dirai-je Maman"
("Twinkle, Twinkle, Little Star")
K. 265

Wolfgang Amadeus Mozart
(1756–1791)

THEMA
[Andante]

VAR. I

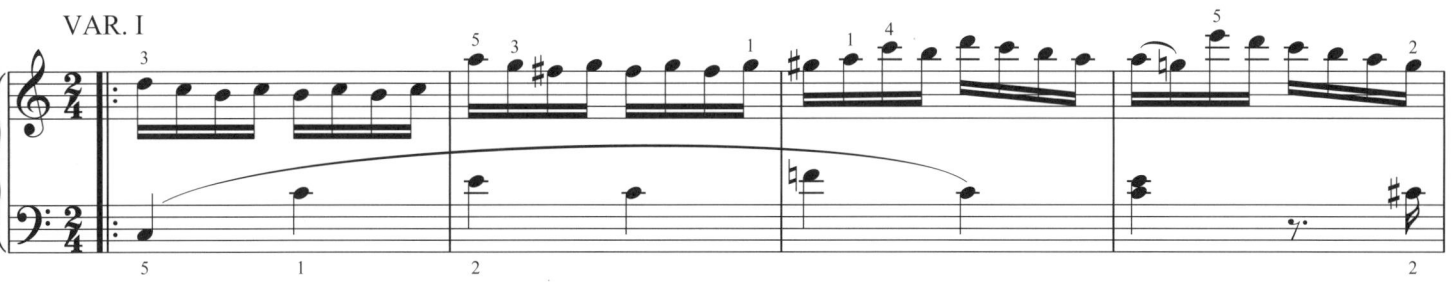

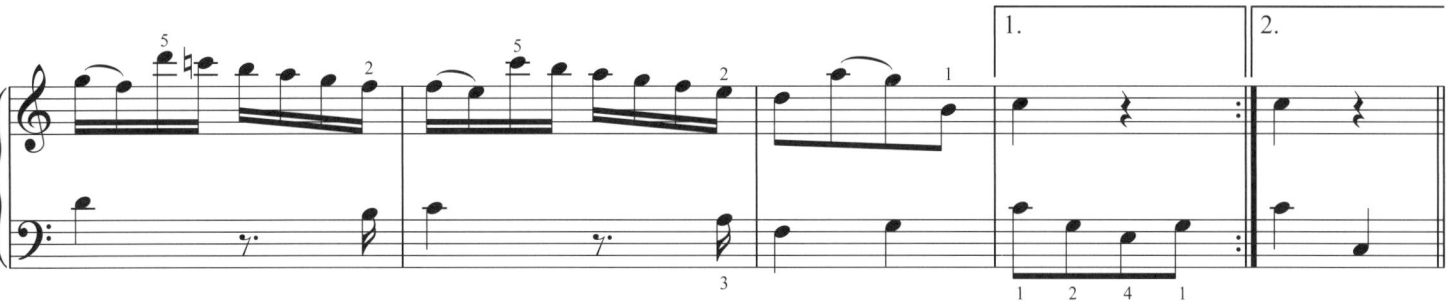

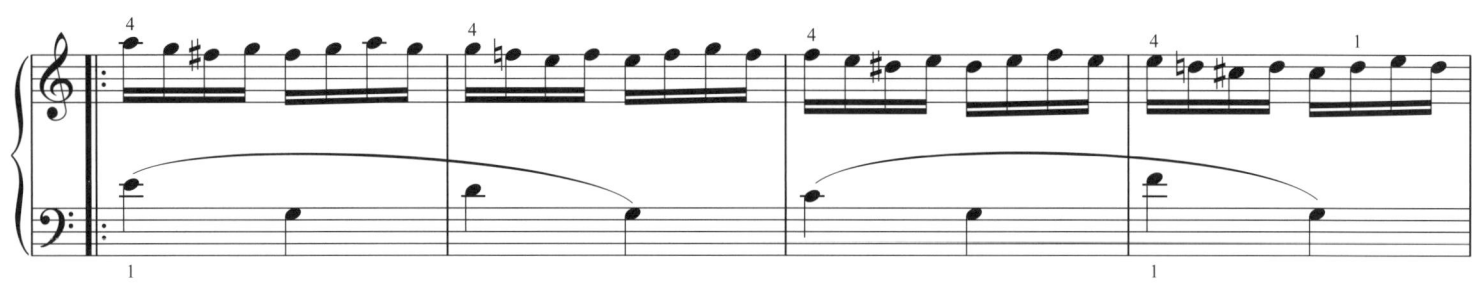

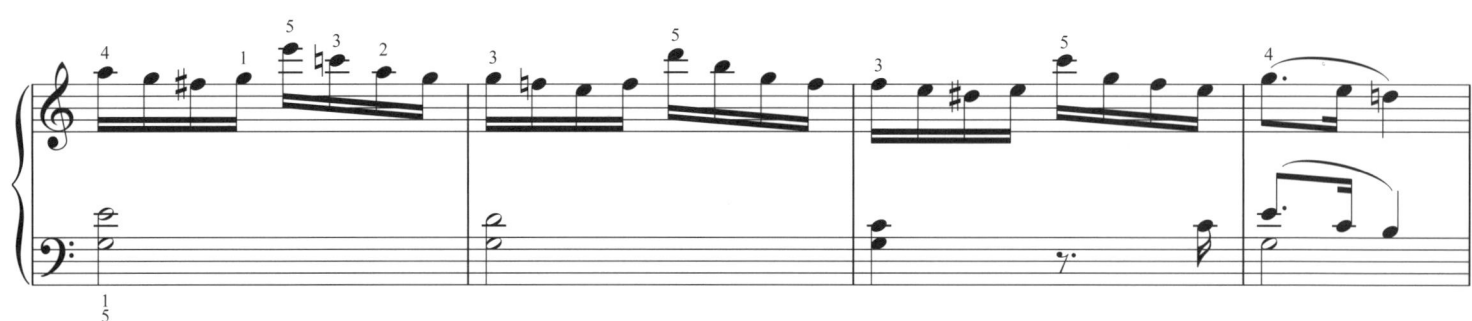

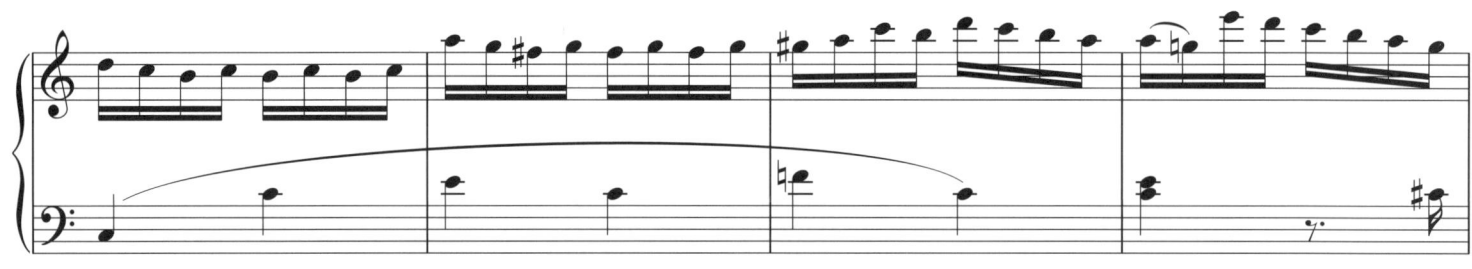

VAR. II

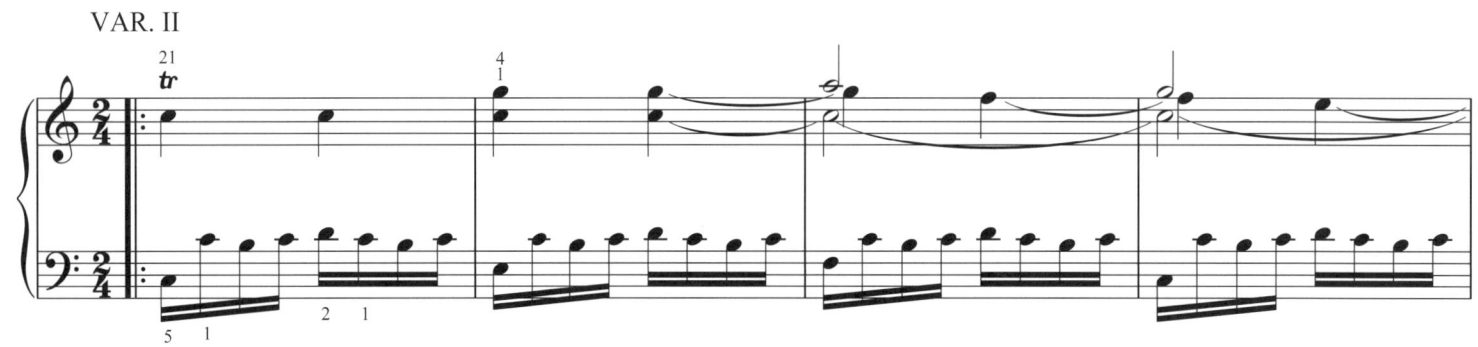

VAR. III

VAR. IV

VAR. V

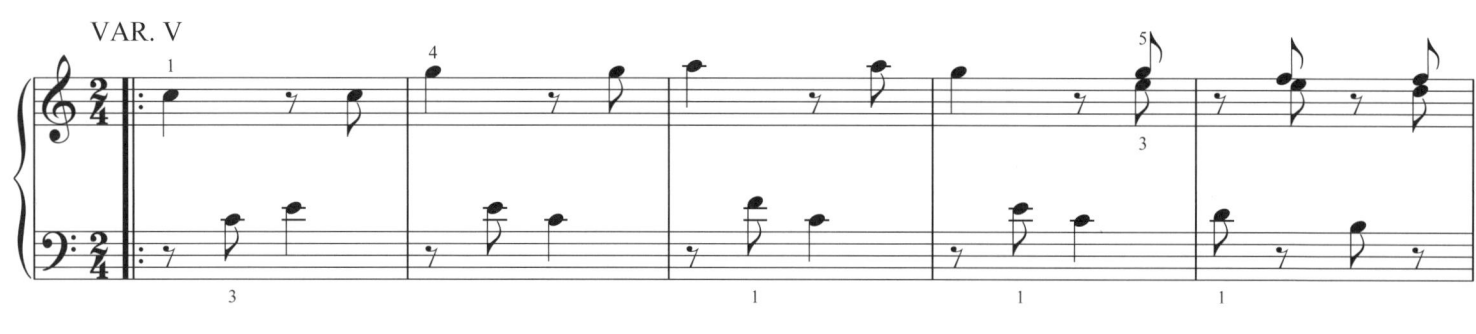

VAR. VI

VAR. VII

VAR. VIII

VAR. XI

Adagio

VAR. XII

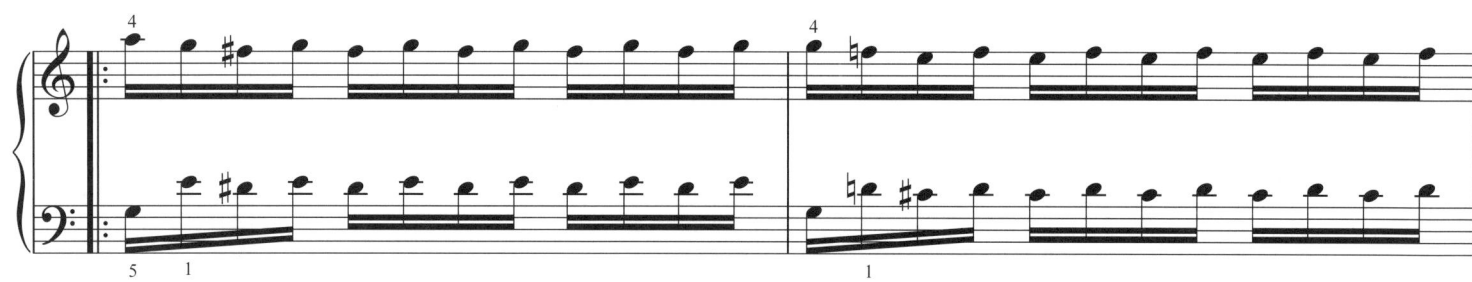

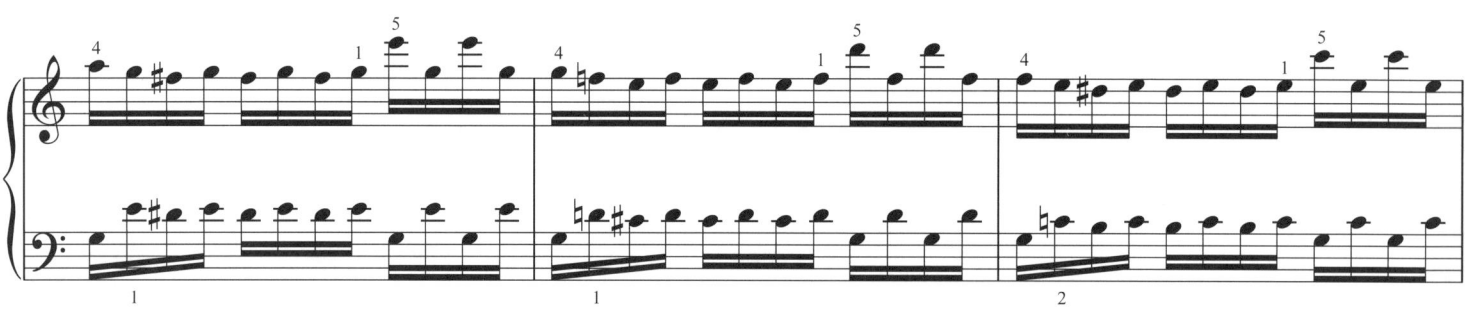

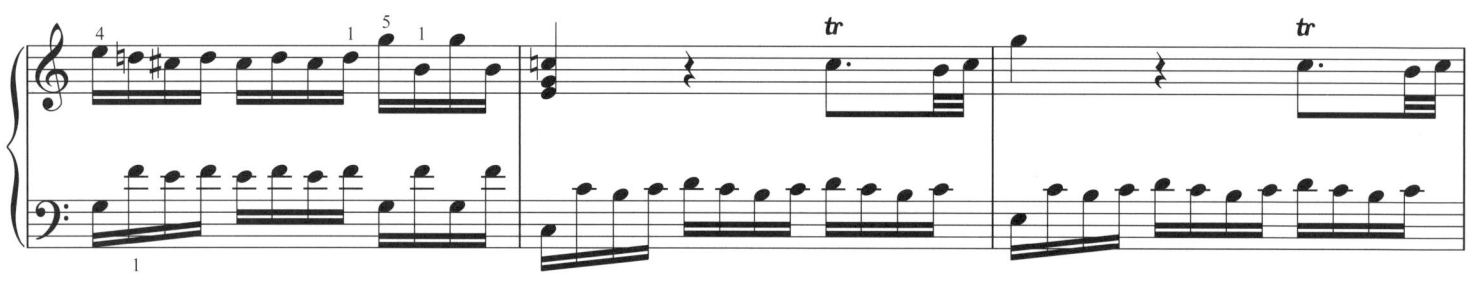

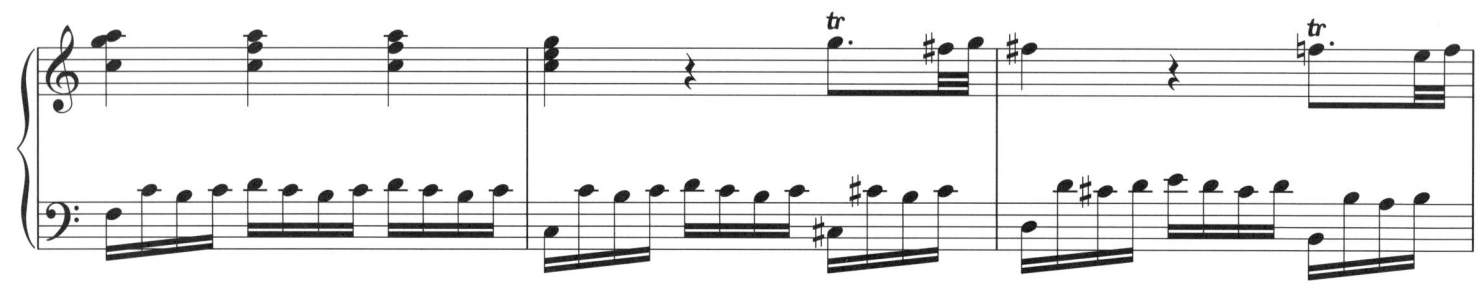